SITUATING SOUND AND RHYTHM
(MUSIC OF TAMIL NADU)

SITUATING SOUND AND RHYTHM

(MUSIC OF TAMIL NADU)

T.V. Kuppuswami

GYAN

GYAN PUBLISHING HOUSE

NEW DELHI-110002

SITUATING SOUND AND RHYTHM
(Music of Tamil Nadu)
(Music)

ISBN : 81-212–0607-3

Published in 1999 in India by
Gyan Publishing House
5, Ansari Road
New Delhi-110002

Laser Typesetting at : Computer Services,
Printed at : Mehra Offset Press, New Delhi

CONTENTS

Acknowledgements

Most important debt is owed to all writers (past and contemporary) upon whom I had drawn heavily.

To musicians, musicologists, historians and friends for critical observations.

To Mrs. Lakshmi Kuppuswami, T.K. Venkatasubramanian and Mrs. Chitra Seshadri for the noble battle fought for refinement of views.

To Mrs. Girija Venkatasubramanian for helping in the preparation of the manuscript and for sharing typing burden.

M/s Gyan Publishing House for the publication of this study with patience and accuracy.

T.V. KUPPUSWAMI

Delhi
25, March 1999

Prejudice and Pride

Reviewing my book *Carnatic Music and the Tamils* Matthew Allen of Duke University wrote "Carnātic music is the classical art-music of South India. It is simultaneously a virtuoso performance tradition of 'absolute music' revelling in pure SOUND and a Hindu devotion tradition in which Sāhityam (text) is extremely important....the majority of song texts in Carnātic music...have been composed in the Sanskrit and Telugu languages...Most scholars of Carnātic music view the long tradition of treatises in Sanskrit as their primary intellectual heritage and revere without any linguistic clues to help the reader follow the narrative disjunctions." These observations are thought-provoking and show that a book review can widen the canvas than simply highlight professed inadequacies. The need for 'Situating Sound and Rhythm' is obvious.

The musicographic reflections that follow are occasioned or rather provoked by the disproportionate (linguistically) theory in the discipline (musicography) as compared to the veritable welter of theoretical writing in general history, sociology and epistemologically oriented philosophy. This undertaking is neither meant to be an introduction to the basic facts of Carnātic music history, nor intended as a textbook of historical method. Still less, does it constitute a philosophy of history or an ideological critique in the traditions of Hegel or Marx. For decades now musicologists have been talking about a crisis in musicological thought. This work is not intended to make good the loss but bears the semblance of music orthoepy, mostly reflections of someone directly involved in the field and not those of a philosopher standing above it all. It arose not from ambitious theoretical lucubration but as response to survey glances (reviews of my books). I endeavour to provide an acceptable kiosk.

Since perusing my present publication the reader may wonder why some difficult sounding terms are brought to bear on music. If that happens, I understand it, since the academic field of musicology is yet to be influenced by such terms (norms) of assessment. All acquisition of knowledge follows (indeed must follow) an underlying pattern of objectification and assimilation. Music historians are of course historians like any others. But their field is complicated by the nature of music as an art. In some instances, music composers behave as historical chroniclers. But when we speak of the meaning of a piece of music, composers become subjects. The composer remains as a subjective agency behind his work. This again may sound a philosophic premise but it serves to bridge the gap between the Tamil savant of Carnātic music and his Telugu, Kannada and Malayalam counterparts. It appears to me that many non-Indian reviewers are swayed by hearsay of the idealistic tradition of Carnātic music in Tamil Nadu. This is an instance of 'Reception history'.[1]

Reception historians habitually distrust the distinction between appropriate and ill-conceived views of musical works. Nevertheless they are reluctant to dispense entirely with criteria for selecting and classifying the modes of reception lest they find themselves adrift in a sea of relativism. Is it a foregone conclusion that a history of reception is a process that lends itself to narration at all, rather than a mere accumulation of data that fall into no discernible pattern? The twin problems that arise are how to substantiate opinions? and how to cast changing modes of reception into coherent history? A methodological solecism to mingle or confuse normative judgements (postulates as what ought to be) with descriptive ones (knowledge of what used to be) becomes unavoidable.[2]

Art is historical solely on the basis of separate and individual works considered on their own merits and not by virtue of their external relationships, let alone the influence they supposedly exercise on each other.[3] To reach an agreement on a permissible amount of abstraction that would save music history from suffocating in details without being so far removed from individual works, it is also felt necessary to draft a history of musical techniques. The productive forces of music (particularly after the advent of the Nāyaks and Marāṭṭās at Tanjore, Tamil Nadu) lead to controversies. Whenever, in the course of history one area of the techniques is developed in isolation, others invariably remain backward giving lie to progressive features by undermining the unity of the work. Tamil Nadu had altogetherly a different experience. Tamil tradition (indigenous) was not overthrown, but new forces were assimilated.

A particular fragment of musical reality varies according to the period, field or genre studied. Scholarly experience has shown that it is not possible virtually in every instance to determine to the satisfaction of everyone concerned, whether a particular result is interesting and relevant or weak and misguided. Any controversy raised will remain pointless until it can draw upon those practical examples and experiences without which proposed scholarly theories will be devoid of meaning and be numbers in statistical tables. It remains uncertain to what extent a historian is to regulate his selection and ordering of facts to conform to the modes of thought and habitual patterns of outlook that reigned in the age which he ventures to depict.

What is attempted is the history of an art form. On the one side it is flanked by the dictates of 'aesthetic autonomy' and the other by a theory of history that clings to the concept of continuity.[4] With some leeway in chronology and some stretching of fact it can safely be said that art theory was based in the sixteenth and seventeenth centuries on the relationships of compositional techniques to social function; in the seventeenth and eighteenth centuries on the 'affections' (objects represented in music) ; in the eighteenth and nineteenth centuries on the structure of self-contained works.[5] In the past twenty five or thirty years the doctrine of affection has been superceded by the aesthetic of expression and this in turn by structuralism as the dominant view in art theory. Yet, the old survives alongside the new. A view accepted by a group of persons whom a consensus of social opinion deems qualified to pronounce judgement, does not always imply that it is more widely held than the other. Monographs on composers, structural analyses of fragmentary works, brief histories of various genres and picturesque extracts from cultural, intellectual or social histories form grist to the mill.

The present attempt seeks to reconcile the 'autonomy aesthetic' with a 'sense of history'. Art-history depends on the historian's knowledge of the treatises so that Art-history may not become an ad hoc arrangement imposed upon arts and art-works from outside. Indigenous sources in Tamil as well as treatises in Sanskrit and Telugu have been studied and quoted so that 'narrative disjunctions' are kept at a minimum. Works on music and performances, the environment surrounding the lives of composers who wrote them, the structure of the institutions for which they were intended, the aesthetic idea of the age and the social strata that sustain musical genres have all been considered. Historical awareness in the music field is an established fact. Many accredited compositions in Telugu, Sanskrit and Kannada ianguages are popular with the exponents of the art in Tamil Nadu. Compositions in Tamil are equally popular. The discovery of 'the subjective agency' in the music history of Tamil Nadu leads to 'music'. 'Carnātic music' maintains its identity throughout thereby registering an unbroken continuity. This picture of the past cannot be disintegrated into unrelated fragments. The rule of the Nāyaks and Marāṭṭas at Tanjore is a political event, but the 'musical event' is not a departure from the past. Religion played a significant role in strengthening time-honoured beliefs. The temples, maṭhas (monasteries) and saint composers kept the torch aglow. Music and religion are inseparable entities whether the tenets find expression in Sanskrit, Telugu or Tamil languages.

The genesis and progress of the system of Carnātic music are traced by most of the musicologists to Sanskrit, Telugu and Kannada sources. The system was adopted by Tamil, Kanara, Malayalam and Andhra regions.

In other parts of the world rationalisation of music had taken a different path. The complex determinants that made adoption of Carnātic music are unique and can be summarized. Thoroughly concrete characteristics of the external and internal situation of the temples and mathas, the results of sociological influences and religious history, allowed a rationalism which was peculiar to monarchies of Tamil Nadu which foster progress of music mostly technical in character. The rationalisation of music, dance and other allied arts, the origin of the music forms which resulted from certain forms of social life at Tanjore, and finally the adoption of the Vīṇā and later violin led to the unimpeded progress of 'classical music' and its spread among the bourgeoise. It has its roots in the specially religious character of the Tamilians. It is to be remembered that the indigenous and the incoming co-mingled and flow as a single stream.

25, March 1999 T.V. Kuppuswami

REFERENCES

1. It can be noticed (at times) that even polemical and propagandistic upsurge of interest in what is called the 'The History of Impact and Reception'. The former term emphasises the object that sets the process in motion, the latter the public towards which that process is directed.
2. An incontrovertible fact is that European music history since the Renaissance has advanced under the banner of what Alfred Einstein once used on a book title 'Greatness in Music' (New York, 1941).
3. Theodre W. Adorno: Aesthetic theorie (Frankfort am Main 1970), p. 263.
4. *Aesthetics* is the science of expression in 'Art of cognisable beauty'. *Aesthetic phenomenon* can be expressed and communicated. The history of the genesis of art-form is accomplished by reciprocal accommodation of means and ends. The final meaning of the whole emerges from 'Changing relationships'. Art-forms are emotional representations and throw coloured light on emphasis. They attain a character which clearly distinguishes them from other happenings. *Artistic pleasure* attaches not to the materials of the works of art as such to their form. *Aesthetic nature* is the specific essence of the art. Ability of art to satisfy needs is rooted in its very nature.
5. Two kinds of appeals are cognisable in the field of music. They may be termed as 'Primary' (direct) and 'Secondary' (indirect). There are varieties of gradual transitions between the primary and secondary appeals. *Creative artistry* involves an intuitive mind. Historical memory serves as the background material for such an artistry. *Aesthetic experience* is inferred from the nature of its manifestations and the means of its achievement. This link between history and artistry heightens the timbre of aesthetic experience. *Historical contextuality* of an art-study constitutes an aspect of its comprehension accessible to cognition. Influencing factors may be termed as 'Extra musical'.

1

Datum and Facts

Art is a complex subject of scientific enquiry and *aesthetic cognition* at each stage of its development is a fundamental problem. Art is often called 'The study of man' or 'The science of the human soul'. It appeals to emotions and senses as well as to the intellect. For some, art is simply entertainment, whereas others see it as an essential part of the spiritual life. Some look for depth and dignity in it; others for an easy form of distraction. Some appreciate that art enriches personality, strengthening a person spiritually and mentally; while others see it as something intended to brighten up their leisure hours. The practice of applying both aesthetic and ethical criteria in evaluation had become deep rooted. Poet Rabindranath Tagore observes, "Art reveals man's wealth of life which seeks its freedom in forms of perfection which are ends in themselves. The world as an art is the play of the Supreme person revelling in image-making. If we make an attempt to capture life as expressed in living tissue we may find carbon, nitrogen and many other things utterly unlike life—but never life itself through its material ....We may call it 'Māyā', but 'Māyāvin' (artist) is not hurt. Art is 'Māyā,' it has no other explanation, but it seems what it is[1]."

Tagore also declares that, "Music is the most abstract of all arts as mathematics is in the region of science... pure essence of expressiveness in existence is offered in music. In sound, it finds the least resistance and has a freedom unencumbered by the burden of thoughts and facts. It gives it a power to arouse in us an intense feeling of reality, it seems to lead us into the soul of all things and makes us feel the very breath of inspiration flowing from the supreme creative joy... In music, the feeling exacted from 'sound' becomes an independent object itself. It assumes a tune-form which is definite, but a meaning which is indefinable and yet grips our mind with a sense of absolute truth. After all, art is the response of man's creative soul to the call of the real. It is a solitary pedestrian who walks alone with the multitude continually assimilating various experiences unclassifiable and uncatalogued."[2]

Dance is an emotional self-expression which gains the status of a spiritual art. Ṛgveda describes 'Uṣās' (Goddess of Dawn) as being clad in gay raiment like the dancer.[3] Dances of Śiva, Kāli, Kṛṣṇa, Gaṇeśa (Vināyaka) and the classical apsarā maidens are described in literature. The arts (music and dance) were essential parts of rituals as envisaged by the Brāhmaṇas and Gṛhyasūtras. Kapila Vātsyāyan writes, "Such a high place could have been given to artistic expression only in a culture where life was regarded as a continual opportunity for the expansion and cultivation of feelings and emotions through which release and salvation were possible, if one willed it here and now... All the arts; not those specifically music and dance, became the most important instruments for the cultivation of feeling... the discipline which these arts embodied in themselves was given value, not only in the realm of aesthetics but also in the realms of religion and spiritual thought."[4] Manmohan Ghosh, on the other hand holds the view that, "Hindu plays were danced and in them rhythm and lyrical elements preponderate and there is little realism or action."[5] This view ignores the link between 'culture' and 'art'. Art in general, and music and dance in particular have always been allies and illuminators of religion. 'Saṅgīta' is regarded as a charming and easy path of yoga. Hindu gods and goddesses are inseparably associated with fine arts. Goddess Saraswatī is portrayed as playing on the Vīnā.[6] Natarāja (an aspect of Śiva) is the deity of dance. Dakṣiṇāmūrtī plays on the Vīnā. Kṛṣṇa is the divine flute-player. He not only danced 'Rāsa' (Rāsa-krīṭai) but also danced on the head of the serpent Kāliyā. Śrīmad Bhāgvata Purāna describes Nārada as singing, playing on the Tānpurā (drone), the music intensifying his devotion and devotion intensifying his music.[7] Sage Vālmīki in the epic Rāmāyana describes Śrī Rāma as a supreme musician.[8]

Like many other mysteries of the universe, 'aesthetic experience' has to be inferred from the nature of its manifestations and the means of its achievements.

A work of art can be understood only from within itself. But its existence can be explained by many circumstances that lie outside it. Freedom of an artistic value coincides with aesthetic value and practical values too. The language of music forms a new level of freedom at which human activity overcomes the distance between 'nature and artistic material'. The process is infinite. Man began imitating nature and ended in transcending 'nature'. From 'imitation of nature' he passed to the stage of 'picturisation of nature' (seen) and finally transcended into the creation of the unseen. Art is the divine superstructure built on the ground-work and basement of nature. Art does not merely imitate reality. It idealises, transfigures and divinizes reality. Art seeks to express intuitions by adequate symbols. Music is the most subjective of all arts and helps man to free himself from the tyranny of nature. Wonderful human voice is the medium of music to begin with. It is adequately responsible to man's urge for creativity. It appeals to the universal and divine element in man. "Art charms us like a loving, youthful and beloved wife" (Kāṅtasaṁmita).[9]

The field of art is unique because: (a) Theories that have stood the test of time are retained in the structure of new knowledge in a completely open and relatively independent rather than in a sublated form. (b) Theories (that are made use of) are subject to the impact of culture of new times are reinterpreted and acquire a new meaning. (c) Some old theories prove to be extraordinarily dynamic in the movement of new critical thought. (d) Art deals with the 'limited and unlimited' and the 'process of comprehending the great values' produced by mankind is infinite.[10] (e) The progress of scientific thinking on art and the status of art in culture show that they form a unity. (f) Historical contextuality of an art-study constitutes an aspect of its comprehension accessible to cognition. This emphasises the need for including the previous results of the pursuit of art.

Rājaśēkhara's *Kāvya Mīmāṁsa* makes Lord Śiva himself the founder and teacher of aesthetics.[11] Nandīkēśvara is regarded as the patron god and progenitor of Indian aesthetics. Kaśyapa and Vararuchi are said to have left works on aesthetics which are not available to us now. Great Indian aestheticians and metaphysicians realised (spiritually) and taught (explicitly expressed) that the human soul like the 'universal' is a part (aṁśa) of the external, immortal, infinite bliss (Ānanda) of the divine love. Personal illumination was sought most frequently through exercise of devotion, religious fervour and obedience.

Anthropomorphic art played a large part in devotion too. As succeeding worshippers and art-lovers worshipped or admired these works, they felt tangibly the thought-forms and in response increased their number. This never-ending chain of cause and effect heightened the aesthetic effect of these art-works and they became not only master-works of genius but powerful centres of the very aspirations they were meant to portray. "Art is related to life as much as mathematics is related to discovery, that is as direction-finder and foreshadower of things to come." Though highly individual, aesthetics incessantly changes with personal consciousness and public opinion. From the anthropomorphic worship, that is external, to the equally selfish desire for personal psychism, 'Aesthetic experience is not ours to hold'. Therefore the expression 'aesthetic' often includes (i) the study of qualities perceived in works of art and (ii) the study of mind and emotions in relation to the sense of beauty.[12]

Literature on aesthetics largely rely on factual materials of the natural sciences, physics taking a place of primary importance. Such studies calculated to ensure clarity, are not without drawbacks. In view of the specificity of man's aesthetic relation to the world in which he lives, a human transformation is achieved and this process is not within the purview of the natural sciences. There seems to be profound wisdom in the statement of Charles Darwin that 'the scientist needs constant systematic contact with art'. Lack of aesthetic taste weakens the emotional side of character which distards the development of mental capacity. Aesthetic element reflects, retracts and focuses all other needs of man. The satisfaction of needs is normally reduced to a definite physical state of 'aesthetic pleasure'. Generation of aesthetic pleasure does not consist in creating new artistic images but in developing the consumer's imagination and creative abilities of imaginative thinking.

Art at times develops sensuous contemplation. Yet, it may not be appropriate to reduce the impact of art to the development of creative abilities. Impact of art facilitates not only the understanding of art specifically (perceived sensual phenomenon) but also abstract theoretical activity. This compels reinterpretation of accumulated individual experiences and draws conclusions that may prove to be quite far-reaching and often in no way connected with the phenomenon perceived. Aesthetic phenomenon is at once expressed and communicated. It is objective reality completely fulfilled by the subject. But subject and object are bracketed inseparably. A truly artistic subject expresses itself; its way of thinking, sensibility, conception of form, and understands the world as the indispensable substratum of its experiences. The experiences are projected onto realities and experience actuality by adopting them. This is spoken of as dialectical relationship between subjectivity and objectivity. It is claimed that without it every reflection of reality would remain artistically irrelevant and the very statement of intimacy (anubhūti) would be inarticulated. Jean-Paul Sartre sees the downright criterion of dialectics and he defines it as 'the simultaneous spiritualisation of the external and externalisation of the inner.'[13]

A confrontation between the conscious and unconscious motifs thus arises. They form the bases of art-work. Sometimes, there is a synthesis of these motifs and a balance between spontaneous and artistic inspiration. The conscious and unconscious sectors of the psyche do not form compartments which are totally divided. The history of the genesis of art-form is accomplished by reciprocal accommodation of means and end, desire and ability, flexibility and intransigence of talent. It starts from an anticipated delineatation and from whole details which usually arise by chance and which are loosely connected. The final meaning of the whole emerges from changing relationships. The idea in art is asserted only in conjunction with its realisation. The inseparability of form and content, subject and object, will and ability, contain the key to the understanding of the genesis and development of all cultural forms. Elements which are decisive for the qualitative value of a work are so unstable, and so precariously balancing, that even in the case of the most important products we have often to ask whether effort and mastery or luck or happenstance were responsible for the success.

Evolution of models, marks the starting point of the formation of aesthetic tradition. This may serve as a methodological starting-point. Non-traditional approaches, though significant inevitably are to be methodologically and logically secondary. For instance, the primitive artiste is not only nameless but also faceless. He seems to have been indifferent to his individuality expressing his 'tribal societal norm rather than himself'. His creativity had been conservative. Primitive ritual mementomori is perceived properly as artistic at different times in different regions of the world. In modern times the products of the primitive man's ritual, representational activity acquire universal aesthetic significance and the status of universal artistic value in the consciousness of mankind. Art-form is born as an individual and later on acquires an entirely professional hue. Subsequently, it faces a long period of development and formation ; of emergence of new kinds and genres of artistic creativity—of new varieties of art. The rate and quality of innovation in professional art are determined by concrete historical conditions. Inevitably, they differ from epoch to epoch and the emergence is slow and gradual.[14]

Beauty is an innate and inherent passion of any human being. Sense of the beauty is inherent in man since man seeks to know himself and master the nature. He has a passion for the disinterested pursuit of 'Truth' for its own sake. As per Hindu philosophy, man had a passion to rise above *Tamoguṇa* and *Rajoguna* and give a free play to his *Satvaguṇa*. With intuition stimulated, he is able to sense beauty of the universe in a spirit of detachment and delight. This fosters the desire to behold 'the Beauty of God' (a rare and peerless experience) and hear the 'Music of the spheres'.

Aesthetics is the science of expression in art of the 'cognizable beauty' of the universe. Despite the claim that the search for beauty is an inherent passion in human beings ; only a few have the instinct for cognizing visions of beauty and expressing them in one fine-art or other. All others perhaps could appreciate what is presented before them. They form the group of *Rasikas* (Sahṛdaya).

A subjective and intuitive element is involved in the cycle and hence aesthetics prove elusive. Rhythm, symmetry and harmony, proportion, beauty, grace, etc., are external manifestations of inner spiritual experience. The link between internal experience and external manifestation forms the soul of aesthetics.[15]

Plato, the well-known Greek philosopher emphasized that 'Our love of what is extremely beautiful is due to our heart's search for the absolute and archetypal beauty. Aristotle, his pupil, held art 'to be an imitation of nature though the aesthetic notion is pure, disinterested and universal'. In medieval and modern western art, artistes and aestheticians attempt to pass 'beyond the seen'. Gothe says that, 'Beauty is inexpressible....It is a hovering, fleeting and glittering show whose outlines elude the grasp of definition'. Schelling says that art conducts us from the 'vestibule of reality into the innermost shrine' and reveals 'the transcendental to our vision'. To him 'Art is its own authority and is original and creative'.

Our scriptures prove that 'life in the individual in its ontological aspects is but ceaselessly striving for never-ending unalloyed bliss—external, immortal, perennial bliss'. Self-realisation, self-awareness or total self-experience *Aparoksānubhūti* is the summum bonum of human existence. *Ātmachaitanya Samādhi (Aparokṣhagṇana)* is possible only when the mind becomes *sātvik*. Rightly did the sages proclaim 'Mind alone is the cause for Man's release from bondage' *(Mana eva manuṣyānām kāraṇam bandha mōkṣayō)*.

The artiste occupies a special position as such. He is not a seer, but he has occasional glimpses of the orders that lie at the heart of things. He is sometimes compared with a seer (Muni) perhaps on this account. The sensitive mind of the artiste is inspired by typical facts of nature. Overcome by excitement and joy of the vision, he shares it with others. He transforms the vision using his imagination and it serves as the symbol of perfect beauty created by the artiste, they get a glimpse of the cosmic beauty which the artiste had the privilege to have. They experience what is termed as 'analogous-delight'. Such a process of transmission presupposes that the *Rasika* is of the same mental make-up as that of the artiste (Sahṛdaya).

Looked at from this angle the artiste serves as a 'Bandha' and 'Mukta. In a wider sense all empirical beauty is an expression of the 'ultimate beauty' of the cosmos. The transmitted experience may not be an authentic expression of the 'highest in beauty'. In the ideal realm of art we have 'a reflection of Brahman', that is the 'central inner beauty of the universe'. Exponents of different varieties of fine arts in India vie with one another in interpreting 'Brahman' in terms of the art they pursue. They try to explain the art as the expression of 'Brahman'. Poets and dramatists call it 'Rasa-brahma-Vāda', musicians call it 'Nāda-brahma-Vāda' experts in architecture, sculpture and painting, etc., call it 'Vāstu-brahma-Vāda'. Specialists in music conceive the sound (Nāda) as a revelation of 'Brahman' which they regard as the ultimate in 'Nāda'.[16]

Significance of 'beauty in art' engaged the attention of western philosophers too. Hegel said that 'Beauty is the revelation of the mind through sensuous forms'. The French philosopher, Prere Andre said that, "There are three kinds of beauty: Divine beauty, natural beauty, and artificial beauty". Didoret said that "Art cannot always imitate 'nature' because 'nature' is always changing and art suggests more than it could express." A.C. Quantrimere De Quincey remarks that, 'Beauty is only a tangible form of the true and the good'. Levegere states, "The whole world is the work of an absolute beauty which is only the cause of things by the love it puts on to them".

Indian philosophers make use of concepts like *Ramaṇīya*, *Chāru* and *Chāruta*; and *Chāruta, Sundara* and *Soundarya* express contours of beauty. The oft-quoted 'Satyam, Śivam and Sundaram' express the essence of the concept of the unity of Truth, Goodness and Beauty. The Lord is *'Sat, Chit, Ānanda'* (Being, Consciousness and Bliss) and this illustrates truth, goodness and beauty as aspects of spiritual bliss (Ānaṅda).[17] Words like *Ramaṇīyaka, Soundarya* (attraction) and *Chārumata* (loveliness) can be taken as equivalents of the English word 'beauty'. It is called 'Aḷaku' in the Tamil language. The well-known Sanskrit author Māga says: "The beautiful is what charms us in new ways moment after moment."[18] The most renowned Sanskrit dramatist Kālidāsa says: "In our enjoyment of art, there is also an element of renaissance due to our experience of beauty in our births."[19]

Finite beauty is an aspect of the 'infinite' and 'absolute' beauty of God. Artists are creators of loveliness and give us creations rivalling and surpassing the loveliness of nature.[20] Manmata says that: "The speech of the poem creates a world which is not fettered by the laws of destiny which is the very essence of joy that is self-existent and non-dependent on anything else and brings into existence a creation glittering with the nine Rasas."[21] Any discussion of the significance of art presupposes the understanding of beauty in art. The content of a work of art—its ideal is a product of the artist's imagination. Yet, it is not unreal or illusory. Hence, ontological considerations seem to be irrelevant to the character of art. Probably, this realisation made the Indian philosophers believe that for a proper understanding of the character of beauty in art, it is necessary to separate this branch of investigation from philosophy proper and entrust it to another class of thinkers equally inte rested in art but not committed to any metaphysics.

Since problems concerning the character and significance of art are closely associated, the sectors 'Alankāra' and 'Darśana' in the treatment of art, though distinct often run into each other. Many who started as Alaṅkārikas and studied the structure and function of art were drawn into deeper problems of its meaning for life. Some, who were basically philosophers and yet were concerned with the significance of art turned their attention to the 'nature of art'. As a result, philosophical enquiry came to admit two branches, of which one confines to the 'nature of beauty'and another to artistic beauty.

Beauty may be said to be perfect when it is untainted by any association with ugliness and when it is unaffected by any change either in the object itself or in the disposition of the subject. This is rarely to be found in nature and hence we turn to art. Art is the human portrayal of the ideal of 'perfect beauty' which the mind entertains. Hence artistic beauty is complete; it is constant; it is immune to changes subjective or objective. The physical medium that art employs may undergo change or mutilation. But the idea it represents survives the ravages of time. That is why even fragments of ruined monuments or parts of the forgotten play are valued. They enable us to reconstruct and enjoy the idea behind them. Appreciation too, could only be impersonal ; the enjoyer *(Rasika)* rarely reviews the object from the utilitarian angle. Thus the secret of the success of artistic beauty over natural beauty is that it falls outside the real world. The artist draws material from the world in the form of particular objects or situations and these are transformed by his imagination. The process of transformation has been called 'Generalisation' (Sādhāraṇikaraṇa), by the Indian aesthetician. The pleasure that art yields is referred to as 'Paranivrtti' or (higher pleasure).

Bharata, the author of *Nāṭyaśāstra* elaborated the 'Rasa concept'. To appreciate an emotion indicated by a situation, one has to withdraw into oneself and live through the experience in a sublimated form. Such a process of appreciation is said to yield an order of delight which is more intense than in the other case. Appropriately called 'Rasa' (Literally-'Flavour'), because to know what an emotion is like, one has oneself to taste it. Broadly speaking 'Rasa' means aesthetic enjoyability. Bharata's aphoristic statement sums up this in the Rasa-Sūtra.[22]

By expressing an emotion in a refined form exactly as presented by the artist, the appreciation unwittingly secures emotional culture. In this manner, apart from giving greater delight, the predominantly emotional type of work leaves a permanent impression on the character of the appreciation.

The 'Rasa' school seems to have followed the 'Alaṅkārika' school dealing with figures of speech; the 'Riti' school dealing with style; the 'Vakrokti' school dealing with the indirect, elegant expression of mood ; the 'Dhavani' school dealing with literary suggestiveness and the 'Auchitya' school dealing with fitness and appropriateness of expression. Indian aesthetic development is in the direction of 'Rasa' and 'Dhvani'. It arrived at the doctrine of 'Rasa' in the sector of metaphysics and the doctrine of 'Ātman' in the sector of innermost love of being. To the concept of Rasa, the Dhvani school provided an added grace. Aesthetic elements of Alaṅkāra, Guṇa, Rasa and Dhvani combine to make kinetic and potential 'Vāsana' (impression) of beauty and emotional realisation. The resultant energy of aesthetic enjoyment is the Rasāsvāda (Rasa enjoyment). This aesthetic delight is different from the delight of the senses in which "there is the element of selfishness of impulse and shortage of duration." It is more akin to spiritual bliss, but less intense and less immortal than the 'Ānaṅda' (Bliss of soul). 'Rasa' is the soul of goodness of art, 'Dhavani or Vyaṅgya' is her life, 'Guṇas' are her mental qualities, 'Sabdārtas' are her body, 'Arthālaṅkāra' are her natural ornaments *Śabdālaṅkāras* a are the dress and decoration.[23] Any attempt to exalt one of these elements at the expense of others or exclusion of others will stultify itself.[24]

Closely associated with the concept of 'Ānaṅda' is the concept of 'Rasa'.[25] Just as a white ray of light is refracted by a prism into seven variegated primary colours, the spiritual Ānaṅda shines refracted on 'Nine rasas' in the human mind. Rasa is the aesthetic perception of the "beautiful". Aesthetic joy is disinterested and is super terrestrial (Alaṅkāra). It is therefore more sublime than sensual pleasure. It is considered to be a 'Cognate of Brahmānaṅda'- (Divine bliss).

The Rasa type of art of the Indian aesthetician led to important developments. The concept of 'Dhvani' emerged. Its emergence underlines the fact that emotion could only be suggested or indicated. It cannot be presented directly or described. The analysis of the process by which Rasa is experienced led to different theories on the relation of Rasa to the self on the experience.[26]

Yehudi Menuhin, the internationally famous violinist observes : "Indian music has purity in that it eliminates conflicts and concentrates upon a mood....Western music had built into it changes of mood and conflict. One listens to it largely for entertainment. The Indian approach is one of depth and continuity in time". In listening to and understanding music there are two basic approaches — (a) Our intellectual analysis and (b) Emphatic or sympathetic transference of our perceiving personality into the other sphere. These approaches tend to be mutually exclusive even in the same culture.[27]

Favouring Bhāva (concentration on a mood) as a theme, the Indian artistes brought art into direct contact with religion. A theme of art need not necessarily be religious. But our artistes have not been able to ignore the treatment of the religious sentiment of devotion to God (Bhakti) and the tranquility (Śānti) of liberation. In addition to secular feelings like fear (Bhaya), love (Rati) and sorrow (Śoka). In India, art had functioned as a catalytic agent in fostering religious spirit in an attractive way. The goal of religion is the attainment of *Mokṣa* (liberation). According to Sānkhya school of philosophy, art has no relevance to *Mokṣa*. According to Vedānta, art is more a pointer to and preparation for *Mokṣa*.[28] The harmony which a work of art presents is indicative of the harmony of the universe which an individual who has realised 'Brahman' experiences. The pure delight which it yields especially when it is that intense form 'Rasa', is suggestive of the unsurpassed bliss that characterises the state of *Mokṣa*. No wonder *Rasa* had been described as fraternal to *Brahman* experience.[29] The process of contemplating the beauty of art is virtually a training in meditation (Yoga) which is the key to *Moksa*. Art (music) has the advantage of yoga without involving the strain that usually goes with it. When the theme of art is emotional, it becomes an ally of *Dharma* for providing mental purity.[30]

'Śreyas' and 'Preyas' are antagonistic. But in music both of them meet. 'Śreyas' is that which leads to the external good of man, namely, 'self-realisation.' 'Preyas' is that which is immediately pleasant. What is 'Śreyas' is not 'Preyas'. In music, we find them together. It pleases the ears, treats the senses and tranquilises the mind. Mind and senses are tamed and controlled by it. Music ennobles the soul and reveals the self within.

Products of art being emotional representations of facts and ideas throw coloured lights of emphasis on themes in such a manner that art attains a character which clearly distinguishes it from its counter parts. Every fine art is a human creation. Highest values i.e., Truth, Beauty and Goodness—are all human cognitions. The valuable is that which satisfies human instincts or impulses or certain instincts in their distinctively human form. In art, personality and material clearly make their presence in the end-product. The artiste has to study his material and adapt himself to his way of exposition. He needs different techniques to pronounce words and choose the tune. He identifies himself with the material and imprints his personality on it.

Art, human desire and aspirations clamour for satisfaction. Ultimately what are being satisfied are certain instincts. Instincts are overlaid with human characters. About instincts that fine-arts seek to satisfy there may not be much general agreement. Music or a musical composition may produce a new material or it may bring existing materials in fresh combinations. The Constructive instinct is humanised so as to be synthetic and purposive. They are guided by plans which involve past and future experiences. In fact, fine-arts exist when constructiveness ceases to be used in the interests of practical purpose and exercised for its own sake when satisfaction arises not only from practical success but from contemplation of the product when the created product is enjoyed not for the material qualifications that may attend it but disinterestedly for itself. This is commonly expressed by the saying that "artistic pleasure attaches not to the material of the work of art as such but to its form."

The gratification of the aesthetic impulse includes the pleasure of beauty, a real aesthetic emotion distinguished from the emotions connected with the subject-matter of a musical theme. Every work of art is about something (subject). This subject may excite varieties of emotions. But aesthetic emotion is not one of these emotions as directed in a particular way (artistic way). This is a fresh emotion, a formal one. We often hear of two types of arts, i.e., romantic and classical.[31] This distinction applies to music and dance as well. When we talk of a romantic composer, primarily we recognise some unmistakable flavour or colouring in the composer's music. This has particular relevance to composers who meet the demands of the art of dance. The difficulty in this analysis is to reconcile the type or variety of composition set to music embedding a theme. A romantic art is said to depend for its value on the memorable and exciting ; or importance of the nature of the theme (subject-matter). A 'musical subject' is a part of the 'musical-composition' itself. In this type, the composer proceeds to express himself about what had impressed him.

Indian treatises in the Sanskrit language suggest that in the case of a poet, the more important trait is not learning (Vyutpatti) or practice, but 'Pratibhā' (originality and creative imagination) is defined as 'innate'. (Naisargeeti).[32] Mental power is endowed with the power of visualising new forms and presenting them.[33] A familiar Sanskrit verse describes the creator as a poet and the Universe as it appears to Him. The poet, by the creative power of imagination converts the ordinary terrestrial power of real vision (Lokadharmī) into the super terrestrial power of idealistic-like vision (Nāṭyadharmī).[34] Saraswatī *kanṭabharaṇa* authored by King Bhoja declares : "The poet who creates poetry which is free from aesthetic defects and full of aesthetic merits replete with 'Rasa' will get fame and satisfaction."[35]

Professional skills of composition evince normally a great degree of freedom. They may not develop to the extent of satisfying the musical consciousness of the people. They may not also satisfy well-developed artistic sense. Composing is the art of presenting musical thought in the form of schemata. In it, mechanics of pre-established connections conflict with the organic quality of individual perception. Sometimes an axiologos stamp is also attached and designated as a 'Masterpiece'. A distinctive feature of this quality is uniqueness of the artistic value—that is impossible to evaluate one masterpiece as better or worse than others. 'Uniqueness' is to be taken in the sense of 'Originality'.

In folk-art (the role of the folklore) the guiding factors are principles of normative groundwork transmitted from generation to generation, that is melodic models and rules of intonation. In a given region or village, an average professionalism of its own may emerge while implementing the common traditional heritage. A folk-song artiste (singer) can execute a traditional melody introducing innovations and animating the canon to suit the unique situation of the performance of his mood at the moment. The spectators recognise always the best singers, storytellers, dancers and lamenters. If the structure of artistic value could be interpreted as convoluted history, any masterpiece (folklore, canonic or innovative) convolutes the history of music as a whole in its own way. They may either anticipate it or concentrate in its tradition, or future development or else marking the latest stage of its search.

'Sāhitya' (text) is primarily the coordination of word and sense.[36] On a higher level it also emphasises the companionship of the soul of man and the soul of poetry. A 'Sahṛdaya' (*Rasika* with identical mental disposition) is an emotionally inseparable friend and companion of a poet (Kavi). What an art has in store to convey (upadeśa of art) is like the upadeśa of the beloved (charming, graceful and irresistible).[37] It is claimed that it destroys inauspiciousness (Śiveta nakṣyate). *Sāhityadarpana* claims that art will supply all aims of human life.[38]

There is no consciously organised continuous movement of music in the form of development of sound relation.[39] Creating from memory is considered primitive, since this kind of sound-combination is limited and accidental. Auditory ability is not something monolithic. In different individuals it may be developed or undeveloped. It may be oriented at different stages of overcoming the resistance of musical material. Yet, the common scale of evaluation of all these ranks is specified by the history of musical intonational creativity as a whole. Art is to satisfy the aesthetic needs which inevitably evolve in members of society at a definite stage in its development. Aesthetic nature is the specific essence of art—ability of art to satisfy needs is rooted in its very nature.

Aristotle said : 'The material of art-history resides not in 'praxis' but in 'precis' (creation of form). A sense of nostalgia may hinder clear hind-sight ; but the increased knowledge they provide is not just unnecessary. A bygone musical event or dance is a complex interaction of text, performance and reception. Study of treatises on music and drama pre-supposes the autonomy of the art. The idea that a musical work belongs to history means a sequence of changes and the purpose is not to elevate a second century or third century aesthetic premise. This conscience does not deny that innovations played their role during these epochs. We have very little means of gauging the degree of innovation. A comparison of styles could be attempted by noting the traits that differ. It then becomes possible to outline at least some, if not all.

REFERENCES

1. Rabindranath Tagore : *The Meaning of Art* (*Viśwabhārati* Quarterly. Vol. IV, No. 1, April 1926.
2. *Ibid.*
3. Ṛigveda: III-61.
4. Kapila Vatsyayan : *Culture of Emotions* (Youth Festival Souvenir, New Delhi).
5. Manmohan Ghosh: *Abhinaya Darpaṇa of Nandikeśvara* (1956), Introduction.
6. Vīnāvādana Tatvagya : Sruti-jati viśarata : Tālagñasya prayāsēna mokṣamargam Cha gachchati" Yājnavālkya Smṛti. III. 4. 115).
7. Śrīmad Bhāgavatam: I.6. 38-39.
8. Rāmāyaṇa II. 36.

   "Gāndharva Cha Buvi Śrēṣṭō babhuva Bharatāgraja:
9. Pratāparudreeyam: I.8.
10. M. Bakhtin: Estetika slovesnogo tvorchestva (Tr) (Moscow, 1979), p. 333.
11. Kāvyamīmāṁsa: I

    "The inanimate universe consisting of earth, mind or intellect and psyche, self-consciousness in his lower manifestation (apara bhakti) whereas individual soul in high manifestation (Paraprakṛti) and that the individual soul is a part (aṁśa) of himself. (Ref : Bhāgavat Gīta)
12. *Random House Dictionary of English Language.* (Ed) Lawrence Urdang, (Allied Publishers Pvt. Ltd., Madras, 1975), p. 22.
13. Sartre: Critique. (3.29) p. 66.
14. S. Averintsev: Drevaregreche Akaya poetica mirovaya Literature. (Tr) (Moscow 1981), p. 37.

    T.V. Cherednichenka: K. probleme khu doy hestvennai tsennosh. (Tr) (Issue. 5. Moscow 1983), p. 270.

    He speaks of the evolution of professionalism in musical art.
15. Prof. Knight: *The Philosophy of the Beautiful.* II. pp. 16-17.
16. Saṅgīta (music) is not mere nerve titillation. It is a yoga. (Ref: Śrīpriyā. Composition of Tyāgarāja).

    "Music composed of seven *svaras* is a treasure for the great *Tapasviṅs* who have cooled *Tāpatraya.* (Adhyātmik, Atidaivak, Adibautic) "In Thee! Rama! I perceive the world and merge myself in Thee with my intellect cleared and illumined" (Inta Karṇāmṛtam Yemi-composition of Tyāgaraja in the rāga Bilahari).

17. "Ānkikam, Bhāvam Yasya Vāchikam Sarvavāṅgmayam Āhāryam chaṅdrarātitum nama: Sātvika Sivam".

Let us bow to Lord Śiva whose limbs are the universe, voice is all speech and whose decorative Ornaments are the moon and the stars.

18. Śiśupālavadham of Māgha: IV. 17.
19. Abhijñānaśākuntalam of Kālidāsa: Verse 2.
20. Cf: Dhvanyālokam. (Chowkhamba Edn.) p. 498.
21. Kāvyaprakāśa: I.1.
22. Nāṭyaśāstra: IV.1.
23. Daśarūpakam: IV.1.
24. K.S. Ramaswami Sastry: (1) Indian Aesthetics. (Sri Vani Vilasam Press, Srirengam).

(2) Indian Concept of the Beautiful. (Sri Vani Vilasam Press, Srirengam).

25. Taittirīya Upaniṣad: II. 71.
26. The theory of Bhaṭṭanāyaka based on Sāṅkhya philosophy holds that 'Rasa' is newly produced in the self which in its true nature is immune to pleasure and pain. The theory of Abinavagupta based on general Vedānta represents that 'Rasa' is a manifestation of native bliss of the self.
27. Psychology in Music. (East-West No. 64).
28. As in Fn. 26.
29. 'Brahmāsvādasahodara.'
30. Chitta Śuddi.
31. It is said that good romantic art is 'art that is well begun' and good classical art is 'art well-done'.
32. *Kāvyadārśa* of Dandin. I. 103.
33. Prajñānavanavoṇmėṣaśālini pratibhā mata.
34. Aparē Kāvyasamsāra Kavirēka: Prajāpati:

Yatāsmai rochate viśwān tatedam parvartatē (Dvaṅyālokam. III) p. 498.

35. Nirdoṣam guṇavat kāvyāmālaṅkārai alaṁkṛtam.

Rasānvitam kavi: kurvan kīrtim prītim vidāthi. I:2.

36. Kāvyālankāra sūtras. I.16.
37. Mammaṭa: Kāvyaprakāśa. I.2.

'Kāntāsamhita tayōdeśa yujē'

38. Sāhityadarpaṇa I (Chaturvarga phalaprāpti)
39. B.V. Asafyev: *Muzzykalnaya forma kak protsess* (Tr) (Leningrad, 1971) pp. 311-12.

2
Semantics

Music history requires a pre-existent canon pinned down by tradition, that is a structured account of the past. Aesthetic canon is a premise of music historiography. The problem lies in deciding its scope since we hear of varieties like 'Presentation music' and 'Everyday music'. Presentation music is a phenomenon that has been in existence from time immemorial. It is music which is not a constituent part of some larger extra-musical process but exists as a source of entertainment in its own right. The doctrine of 'Art for art's sake' is a nineteenth century slogan coined by the Bohemians of the royal courts.

The world of Carnatic music is fortunate in having inherited a rich legacy of 'Lakṣaṇa Granthas'. The authors of these granthas have made a scientific and systematic study of art-forms. Classical-arts derive strength and vitality from these treatises (Lakṣaṇa granthas). Such treatises provide the structural framework relating to the rendering of the arts.[1] The treatises provide the means for analytical and critical discussion on the theory and practice of music. These treatises on music are broadly grouped under the heads 'sacred literature' and 'secular literature'. Treatises which are chronologically earlier give primacy of place to dance and drama and devote only few chapters to music proper. Hence they are sometimes classified as 'Nāṭya literature'. Those which belong to the medieval period are known as 'Gīta-Nāṭya literature'. Music proper gains greater attention in this anthology. Works belonging to the modern period are 'Gīta literature' and they deal with the techniques of music.

Music history must proceed from the study of works on music. Even if more is said about the composers whose biographies are scoured for explanatory matters, that of music itself is based on the notion of the 'Autonomy of the art'. Autonomy plays the same role of an explanation sketch as does the concept of 'National spirit' in political histories. Evolution of music-aesthetics then becomes an autonomous and unduplicatable work of art born of itself and existing entirely for its own sake. Thematic and motive manipulations, developmental variation and development of subtle, yet far reaching harmonic and tonal relations are taken as factors of musical logic.

An artiste is sometimes spoken of as an 'Antiquarian'. He is one who is piously absorbed in reconstructing fragments of the past out of an instinctive urge to collect and preserve on the one hand and a desire to escape the pressures of the present on the other. But, this view is sometimes overemphasised. The primary (original ?) motivation of the development of the art of music lies in the urge not to master tradition but to subject it to a rigorous critique. The realisation that a gap exists between the aspirations of the present and the imprint left upon the present by the past, is at the root of it.

In the formation of 'Cultural structures' (compositions for music/ dance/or drama) common ethnic origin and national community are sociologically and culturally, comparatively irrelevant. Every artistic medium of expression contains national characteristics. Every art expresses itself in national idiom. The language of art starts with a national idiom and preserves the national quality inspite of the supernationality to which it aspires. Tyāgarāja for instance, composed in the spirit of his mother tongue (Telugu). Yet we enjoy and value his compositions without being Telugu speaking persons. What seems to be necessary is an ear for Telugu cadence of his diction. However, it must be conceded that without the feeling for the individuality of a language, it is difficult to understand the art-content.

References to music and dance are found in Vedic literature. In the recitation of the 'Ṛchās' employment of sound modulation is patent (Udātta, Anudātta, Svarita). Ṛks are prayers to different gods of the epoch, and the composition of the Ṛchās have been classified into *Hrasva, Dīrgha,* and *Pluta*. This enabled the participants to render Ṛchāś harmoniously. The musical system of the period is described as 'Hrasva Gāyana' or 'Archika system'[2] Ēkaśvarī is distinguished by the addition of new 'notes' to the *Gātic* system. It is probable that there had been an experimentation with various notes before sighting an agreeable note (Svarita Bhāva). Sāmagāna gained shape after considerable trial. Pāṇini and Yājnavalkya admit the use of notes and designate it as 'Āraṇya gānam'. It had limitations.[3] Chants from other sources were used along with Sāma. The resultant scale 'Sāmika' is an admixture. Bharata, the author of *Nāṭyaśāstra*, evidently, had elaborated after analysing those that existed before his time. He is a constructive genius. V. Raghavan who had classified Sangīta literature lists the authors chronologically with brief sketches of their lives and contributions.[4]

Four completely different musical systems of the world are known. They are the classical system, modal system, harmonic system and melodic system. Individually they make use of distinct properties of sound. Yet, it appears that there had been no consciously organised continuous movement of music in the form of development of sound relations. Two categories are cognisable, namely, 'Creativity from memory' and 'Consciously organised continuous movement of music in the form of development of sound correlation.' Creativity from memory is primitive since this kind of sound combination is limited and accidental. (Ref. Ch. 1. Fn. 39).

Classical Indian music is an example of the 'Modal system'. Its characteristic feature is the permanence of a fixed sound called the 'Tonic'. Varieties of intervals could be formed which are further assembled in what may be described as an 'Oblique structure' as it results in an infinite variety of modes (Rāgas). The earliest melody in the Indian system is claimed to be in Sāmagāna. In its developed form, this chant uses the seven notes making a 'Scale', and this forms the basis of development of notes and intervals in a musical scale. The seven notes of Sāmagāna correspond to more or less the same notes now used in the melody scale (Rāga) called Karaharapriyā in the Carnātic system and 'Kāfi thāt' in the Hindustāni system.

It is Ahōbila, who designed a method to arrive at a 'Ratio value'[5]. From these, by use of the cycles of the fifths and fourths and suitable trials several notes and intervals are derived. As many as twenty-two micro-tonal intervals are derived and distributed among twelve notes (Svarastāas). These twenty-two minute intervals are not uniform.[6] These go by the name 'Ēka śruti' (unit interval). By judicious combination of these intervals; twelve corresponding to the twelve notes of the scale are derived.[7] Indian music (current) is based on these twelve intervals (notes) in the scale.

Views differ regarding the pure scale in use during the Vedic period. Some believe that it was the *Bhāvio thāt*, whereas others believe that it was the *Kāfi thāt*. Consensus is in favour of *Kāfi*. A theory of 'Grāma' (Scale), 'Mūrchana' (Modes) and 'Jāti' (species) developed. At first, there were three Grāmas, namely, Sa-grāma, Ma-grāma and Ga-grāma. The last one had been long obsolete. 'Mūrchana' means the rise and fall from and to a particular note of a specific scale. There are three types of Mūrchanas: (a) 'Sampūrṇa' (complete) with all the seven notes of the octave, (b) 'Karah' with six notes of the octave and (c) 'Orab' with five notes of the octave. There are twenty-one mūrchanas; with each of the seven notes of the octave we can have three types of mūrçhanas. Each of the two grāmas have mūrchanas each, fourteen in all. But only seven of the fourteen are in practical use and are known as a 'Jātis'.

In the chapter 'Tatadodyavidi' Bharata stresses the relation between Svaras and Jātis, and the rasas that emanate from the Saptasvaras and Jātis. 'Jāti' described by Bharata is considered as the precursor of the modern Raga. Jāti and Rāga are 'developed' and the 'undeveloped' forms respectively of one and the same concept. According to Bharata, Rāga is what colours and pleases the hearts of all. Popely, the western authority on Indian music defines Rāga as different series of notes within the octave which forms the basis of all Indian melodies and are differentiated from each other from the prominence of certain fixed notes and by the sequence of particular notes.[8] This definition of Popely just explains the technical and special characteristics of the Rāga system.

The word 'Rāga' is derived from the root 'Ranja' which literally means 'to impart colour'. 'Ranjaka' is that which imparts pleasure and happiness and the sense of colouring and emotional tinge are included in it. 'Colour' is connected with 'Form'. Every rāga has an emotional form or colour of its own which differentiates it from others. A rāga is therefore, "That combination of musical notes which has the power to impart colour, that is, which has a specific individuality." Mataṅga defines rāga as, "That special combination of sounds beautified by colourful notes, which charm the heart of the people."[9] Matanga happens to be the only link between Bharata and Abhinavagupta (Abhinavabaratam of 10th century A.D.) or even Sārṅgadeva (Sangītaratnākaram of 13th century A.D.).

Individuality of a *rāga* has two aspects :—(a) *Svaramaya* (musical notes) and (b) *Bhāvamaya* (emotional). *Bhāva* is dependent on *Svara* and *Svara* is dependent on *Bhāva*; they are inseparable. Characteristics of *Jāti* are enumerated since answering the question 'What elements make a combination of notes?' (a distinct structure with individuality).

Jāti-lakṣaṇas as enumerated by Bharata are : 1. Graha (starting point) 2. Aṁśa (the most prominent note infusing life) 3. Nyāsa (concluding note) 4. Apanyāsa (resting point) 5. Bahutva (abundance of certain notes) 6. Alpatva (scanty use of certain notes) 7. Tāra (range of ascend in upper register) 8. Maṅdara (range of descent in the lower register) 9 & 10. Ṣāḍava and Auḍava (use of five/six notes in the ascent; number of notes to be used in the ascending and descending order which may be seven, six or five).[10]

These Jāti-lakṣaṇas are applicable to a Rāga. Terms like Vādi-Samvādi are used to denote consonant, assonant, and dissonant intervals of notes. Some musicologists think that they indicate the most important, comparatively not important and the inimical notes to a rāga. This assumption sounds illogical as it counters the basic meaning of the terms and tends to create confusion. 'Jāti' is comparatively generic and 'Rāga' is specific—this difference is inherent in the two terms. 'Jāti' means a species or class and Rāga is that which colours. Basically there seems to be no difference between the two. Jāti is the first step towards erection of a specific structure of notes and Rāga represents a fully developed stage of specification in musical structures. A rāga as compared with other rāgas is a specific entity. It is so generic as to include various compositions and improvisations within its purview. Compositions differ from one another to some extent. For example, compositions in the rāga Kalyāṇi (Carnātic) presenting individuality through variations is little.[11] Improvisations of ālāpanas (delineations) of a particular rāga by different artistes at different times are not identical. These qualities or combinations of a specific and generic nature differentiate rāga from a single tune or melody. The overall meaning of 'Ranjakatvam' (potential to provide pleasure) is applicable to a simple melody or tune which may sense the emotional colour in a set of notes. Mataṅga gives the derivation of Jāti (root) as that which 'marks the beginning of the experience of Rasa' (aesthetic delight).[12]

Jāti had rightly been called the 'Mother of Rāga' by authors like Mataṅga who are chronologically posterier to Bharata. During the time interval between Mataṅga and Śārṅgadeva (eighth to twelfth centuries) the right perspective seems to have been lost sight of the fact, so much so, we find in Saṅgītaratnākara one composition each attributed to the eighteen Jātis. Later writers identify these compositions with the respective Jātis. This attitude of the authors of the medieval period creates the impression that Jātis were represented in those very compositions which were invariably copied down. This proved fatal to the concept of Jāti. When Jāti turned to be an obsolete concept, development of rāga became obscure. Different systems of rāga-classifications as 'Rāga-rāginī' (Male and female) ; Mela and Thāt were evolved. The relationship between 'Jāti' and 'Rāga' had been kept in abeyance.

Māgha's 'Śiśupālavadha' (a Sanskrit work placed chronologically earlier to Saṅgītaratnākara—eighth or ninth century A.D.) states that ancient rāgas were current during the time. The rāga mentioned in support of the claim is 'Bhinna Sadja' Ratnākaram lists it under Grāma rāgas. Details furnished by Śārngadeva (Ratnākaram) are similar to those furnished by Bharata. Terms like Jāti rāgas and Grāma rāgas become popular. In addition to fifteen Janaka rāgas, Śārngadeva mentions twenty rāgas. To each of these he attaches minor melodies called Bhāsas, Vibhāsas, and Antara bhāsas. The number is optional and not governed by specific rules. Names of Janakarāgas are masculine and those of the remaining three varieties are feminine. Janakarāgas are mostly Grāma rāgas and Upa-rāgas. This group seems to have been left dormant.

The Rāga-rāginī parivāra system of classification between A.D. 1200 and A.D. 1400 is modelled after the existing (then) Bhāsā model of classification: where Janaka rāgas are masculine and Bhāsās, Vibhasās and Antara bhasas are feminine.[13] This classification had been ingeniously designed to help the student of music to have some idea of the interrelation of various scales and 'Rāgas'. Four such schemes which have been popular earlier, are not popular now. The erstwhile system had one possible advantage. It consisted of a limited number of popular rāgas handed down as heritage. Up to the fifteenth century A.D., this system seems to have been quite popular in the northern regions of India.

Attempts to evolve a more rational method are on record since the sixteenth century. Puṅḍarīka-Viṭṭala may be taken as the pioneer.[14] Locana, Hṛdayanārāyaṇa, and others like Śrīnivāsa attempted to usher in scientific orientation. In the Deccan, Vijayanagar rulers made such attempts (A.D. 1550). The 'Mela Paddati' gains momentum. With norms set by Saṅgītaratnākara showing signs of exit, the need for shielding the art of music against corrupt methodologies becomes imperative. In the introduction to the work 'Svarameḷakalānidhi', its author Rāmamātya gives us a picture of the prevailing atmosphere.[15] Evidently Svarameḷakalānidhi is a turning-point in music history.

Rāmamātya is a practical musician and has attempted to reconcile theory and practice of music.[16] He claims to have brought in nearly seventy rāgas under twenty principal scales or melas. Closer scrutiny shows only fifteen melas in his prescriptions. The extra five differ in having 'Chyuta Madhyama Gāndhāra' and 'Chyuta ṣadja niṣāda' for the 'Antara and Kākali notes'. The dividing line between melas is so thin that it is difficult to identify individuality when actually handled. He restates many techniques mentioned in Saṅgītaratnākaram of Śārngadeva. Venkatamakin who succeeds accuses Rāmamātya for misinterpreting some of these techniques.[17]

Inspite of the strictures of Venkatamakin (A.D. 1620) Svaramelakalānidhi is to be respected. It introduces a totally new system of theory and practice. In restating the recommendations of Śārngadeva, it also takes into account the comments of Kaḷḷinātha, the commentator. The work gives a detailed account of the Vīṇā as a standard musical instrument for purposes of demonstration and for playing music. The claim that Rāmamātya saved the Carnātic system of music from Persian influence is genuine.

A spate of music treatises follow the production of Svarameḷakalānidhi. Some of the important works are 'Saṅgīta-darpaṇam' of Chatura Dāmōdara Paṅḍita, Rāgataraṅgiṇī of Lochana, Rāgavibodha of Somanātha, and Saṅgīta Sudhā of Govinda Dīkṣitar. Govinda Dīksitar is counted as 'One of the trio of theoreticians' (others are Rāmamātya and Somanātha). Govinda Dīkṣitar leans heavily on Śārngadeva and makes just few references to Mataṅga, Pārśvadeva and Vidyāraṇya. Since A.D. 1680 the 'Meḷa Prastāra-Paddati' of Veṅkaṭamakin gains primacy.

Veṅkatamakin is the author of the immortal work 'Chaturdaṅḍīprakāśikā'. The work has a summary of the history of music up to the time. 'Mela Prastāra' has the stamp of Bharata's 'Mūrcha-Paddati'. Out of the seventy-two meḷas that Veṅkaṭamakin mentions, just nineteen seem to have been in circulation during his time. He elaborates on nearly fifty-five rāgas under nineteen melas. Veṅkaṭamakin admits twelve notes in a scale and endeavours to prove that his system is based on the twenty-two Śruti system of Bharata.[18] There have been perceptible changes in the names, characters and terminologies of rāgas.

Mēḷas (Parent scales) were enumerated and rāgas classified. 'Saṅgīta Sāra' enumerates fifteen melas with fifty Janya rāgas; 'Rāga taraṅginī' with twelve meḷas and seventy-five Janya-rāgas; 'Svaramēḷakalānidhi' with twenty mēlas and sixty-four Janya rāgas and 'Rāgavibodha' with twenty-three melas and seventy-nine Janya rāgas. Such classifications are not very scientific as they are not based on the individual characteristics of well-defined mēḷas. Names of the meḷas are those of the Rāgas current in those times. Veṅkaṭamakin's improvised classification is more scientific.

According to Venkatamakin, Svaras in an octave are twelve: 'Sa' and 'Pa' are fixed notes, Madhyamas are two, (Śuddha and Prati). Four notes between Śuddhamadhyama and Ṣaḍja, four between Ṣaḍja and top Ṣaḍja, make a total of twelve. If four notes between lower Ṣāḍja and Śuddhamadhyama are taken as two Ṛṣabhas (Ri) and two Gāndhāras (Ga); Ṛṣaba and Gāndhāra could be combined in four ways. In the same manner, if we take four notes between Paṅcama and Dhaivata (Da) and two Niṣādas (Ni), we can derive four combinations. The total (including the two Madhyamas) will be 4 x 4 x 2 = 32 (thirty-two melas) Veṅkaṭamakin did not take the four notes in the lower tetrachord as 'Rsabha' (Ri) and Gāndhāra (Ga). He had not also taken the four notes in the upper tetrachord as Ṛṣabha (Ri) and Gāndhāra (Ga). The four notes in the upper tetrachord as Dhaivata and Ṛṣabha have been ignored.

The 'Notes' envisaged by Veṅkaṭamākin may be listed.[19] 1. Ṣaḍja, 2. Śuddha Ṛṣabha, 3. Suddha Gāndhāra (Chatuśrti Ṛiṣabam, 4. Sādārana Gāndāram (Ṣaḍśruti Ṛṣabam), 5. Aṅtara Gāndhāram, 6. Śuddha Madhyamam, 7. Prati Madhyamam, 8. Paṅchamam, 9. Śuddha Dhaivatam, 10. Śuddha Nisādam (Chatuśṛti Dhaivatam), 11. Kaiśikiniṣādam (Ṣaṭśṛti Dhaivatam), 12. Kākaḷi Niṣādam, 13. Top Ṣaḍjam (upper).

Veṅkaṭamakin affirms that there were only nineteen Prasiddha Meḷas during his time. He is confident that his classification is satisfactory, that he has taken "All the rāgas that are in existence, those that exist elsewhere, and those that may come into existence later." He is sure that every one of the rāgas can be brought under one or other of the seventytwo meḷas.[20] Thirty-six are Śuddhamadhyama meḷas and thirty-six are Pratimadhyamas. Just as a drop of buttermilk would completely change the character of the milk, the change in Madhyamas of meḷas would cause a great difference.[21] The seventy-two meḷas of Venkatamakin are 'Asaṁpūrṇa meḷas'.[22]

'Sangītasārasaṅgrahamu', a Telugu work of a later date makes a classification like the one envisaged by Venkatamakin. But the work treats the melas as Sampūrna.[23] Another work 'Melādhikāra Lakṣaṇa' elaborates on the ideas of Veṅkaṭamakin.[24] Govindāchārya, author of Saṅgrahachūḍāmaṇi adopts Sampūrna mēla system. He devises seventy-two meḷas on twenty-two śṛtis and adopts the nomenclature and norms recommended by 'Saṅgīta-Sārasaṅgrahamu. Goviṅdāchārya had composed lakṣaṇa granthas for the seventy-two meḷas and two-hundred and ninety for Janya-rāgas. The reliance on 'Katapayāthi Saṅkya' had called for additions to nomenclature.[25] 'Chakras' were improvised for easy identification.[26]

Out of the seventy-two melas of Veṅkaṭamakin, forty are 'Vivādi meḷas'. Very few Vivādi rāgas and melas existed before the time of Venkatamakin, as evidenced by available literature. Veṅkatamakin admits that Vādi-Samvādi is essential for rāga-rakthi.[27] T.L. Veṅkaṭarāma Iyer is of the view that when Veṅkaṭamakin evolved the scheme of seventy-two meḷas, he must have taken Rāga as an independent entity and hence his system does not envisage distinction between 'Scale' and 'Rāga'.[28] Veṅkaṭarāma Iyer admits the Sampūrṇa system of Goviṅdāchārya only as 'Scales'.[29] May be that Veṅkaṭāmakin had used terms like 'Janaka rāga' in stead of 'Meḷa'. If we concede that Veṅkaṭamakin's scheme as modified by Govindāchārya is currently followed the meḷas that we deal with are 'scales'.

'Saṅgīta sārāmṛta' authored by King Tulaja of Tanjore estimates the total number of rāgas before the advent of Tyāgarāja and others to be just one hundred and twelve.[30] Even at present rāgas handled by exponents may not exceed this figure. A number of new Janyas with slightly different svarasanchāras in Ārohaṇa and Avarohaṇa are also heard. Great Vākgeyakāras (composers) like Tyāgarāja and Muttuswāmī Dīkṣitar seem to have handled some rāgas popular with the Hindustānī system. In the context, we should also remember that some rāgas mentioned in the Saṅgīta-ratnākaram are still popular with the practitioners of Hindustani music. Till the close of the eighteenth century, the Śuddhasvarasapthaka of Bharata had also been popular with Hindustānī school of musicians. Terminologies of Śuddha and Vikṛutha notes as 'Komala and Teevra' are in vogue for the past four or five centuries. The shift perceptible in respect of Śuddhasvarasapthaka is from Ṣāḍ'ji mūrchanā to Niṣādī mūrchanā of the same scale.[31] Some musicologists attribute this change to the influence of the Natural-scale (śuddha) of western nations which imported musical instruments of various types and shapes from the close of the eighteenth century.

The Śuddha-Vikṛutha svaras of Carnātic music stand rooted to Meḷaprasthāra envisaged by Puṅḍarīka Vittala as early as the second quarter of the sixteenth century A.D.[32] Viṭṭala shifted the traditional Śuddha-stānas (Ri, Ga, Da, Ni) by one svarastāna lower and called them Śuddha-svaras. He named the original ones as 'Vikṛtas' of the respective notes. He made provision for ninety meḷas. He names the notes as 'Paryāya Vṛutya Sūddha' and 'Virkta' for the purpose of completion of the prasthāra. Adopting Vittala's prescriptions many Saṅkīrṇa rāgas appeared. Some Saṅkīrṇa rāgas did exist before his time too. They had become so popular and entrenched that it had not been possible to tamper with them. Consequently, rāgas derived from the meḷas suffered from Vivādi dosa. They gained acceptance because of their inherent pleasing quality (potential).

Chatura Kaḷināta, the commentator of Saṅgītaratnākaram observes "Ri and Ga transgressing the border lines of Triśruti or Catuśruti, the second svarastāna after Śuddha 'Sa' and Śuddha 'Pa' of the Vīṇā ; the third svarastāna which represents Pançamaśruti and Ṣaḍśṛuti (Su-Ga) and Sādhārana 'Ga' in the first tetrachord after Su-Ga; and likewise taking Su-Ni and Kaiśiki-Ni in the second tetrachord after Su-Pa are not scientific (Sāstric).[33] This injunction applies to Nāta and Dévakri rāgas.

This observation of Kallināta suggests that the use of the Vivādi pair of notes in succession had not been allowed. The situation must have changed after Viṭṭala. It is Probable that this change had isolated the mainstream into Carnatic and Hindustānī. Nāṭṭai is one of the melodious of rāgas. It has lent succsur to many subsidiary rāgas. In the tradition of Purandaradāsa (Father of Carṇātic music) any music offering should start with Nāṭṭai rāga. The traditionalists (Dāsakūṭas) commence with the Ūkaboga 'Sadā Gananāta' or with the Kirtanam 'Śaraṇusiddhivināyaka' in the rāga Nāttai.[34] The 'Vakra sañchāra conventions' to rāgas derived from Vivāi-yuktha meḷas have been ignored. It came to be applied to a Sampūrna rāga having no Vivādi svara by adopting one of the Kuṭa-tānas either in the ārohaṇa or avarohaṇa or one tāna for ārohaṇa and the same reverted in avarohaṇa or vice versa thus ushering in a new rāga.[35]

Of the ten varieties of rāgas that Saṅgītaratnākaram speaks of, the first six are Mārgī-rāgas and these have gone out of currency. The last four Rāgānga catuṣtaya must have been current during Śārṅgadeva's time. Eighty rāgas come under this group of which thirty-four were neglected and just fifty-two seem to have been popular. Śārṅgadeva acknowledges that fifty rāgas were derived from Mārgī.[36] Since the advent of Puṇḍarīka Viṭṭala (Mēḷaprasthāra) a new method of rāga classification had come into vogue. There had arisen the necessity to relate rāga to prasthāra. Puṇḍarika is silent about Chatuṣṭaya though he mentions Śuddha, Chāyalaga and Saṅkīrṇa.[37]

Veṅkaṭamakin adopts Chatuṣṭaya classification in a formal way. He has not mentioned precisely the class (group) of each individual rāga but makes mention of 'Rāgāṅga, Bhāṣāṅga, and Upāṅga'. He had not followed Puṇḍarīka Viṭṭala. The 'Mārgī rāga' classification had become obsolete. The Chatuṣṭaya classification too must have gone out of circulation along with the generic one. When Meḷaprasthāra was admitted, the classification into Suddha, Chāyalaga and Saṅkīrṇa is inevitable, perhaps sensible too.

The court musicians of the Marātha King Sahaji I of Tanjore have given (a) Ālāps, (b) Ṭhāyas, (c) Gītas, (d) Śūlatis and (e) Prabhandhas. This would not have been possible unless they learnt and practised them. It is even possible that the Lakṣyas have been memorised by the musicians of the time. We have as legacy hundreds of Kṛtis on the God—Śrī Tyāgeśa composed by King

Sahaji. Several others Sahaji. These are valued as important contributions to the field of Carnātic music.

King Tulaja of Tanjore Marātha line introduces about thirty-six rāgas. Two new rāgas namely, 'Vegavāhinī' (sixteenth mela) and 'Veḷāvali' (twenty-third) are his creations. Vegavāhinī is quite a new rāga's name and its meḷa is an addition to the traditional list of melas. Velāvali is mentioned in 'Saṅgīta Makaranṅtham[38] (Deśī rāgas). Śārṅgadeva makes mention of it and groups it as Naiṣada Jāti of Bharata. Puṅḍarīka Viṭṭala and Sōmanāta assign it to the twenty-ninth meḷa.[39] Rāmamātya, Ragunātha Nāyaka and Veṅkaṭamakin assign it to twenty-third mela. The 'Kanakāṅgi tradition' assigns it to the twenty-third under the name Gaurī-manohārī.

Gaurī-manohārī is considered by Tulaja as a Janya-rāga and is assigned to the fifteenth meḷa. Tulaja lists five Manohārī rāgas namely Īśamanoharī, Gaurīmanōhārī, Dēvamanōhārī, Mādavamanōhārī and Saraswatīmanohārī. All these are his innovations. He seems to have innovated sixteen new rāgas, namely Gaulipanthu, Pūrṇapançama, Māgadi, Śuddhasāverī, Ānaṅdabhairavī, Iṅdugāndāra, Maṇireṅga, Śuddhadeśī, Śrīranjanī, Chāyātaraṅginī, Nāṭakurincī, Mōhanam, Mōhanakalyāṇī, Yedukulakāmboji, Pūrṇachandrika, and Sura-Siṅdhu. These rāgas do not figure in earlier music literature (assigned earlier to his time).

A survey of the contributions made by Tuḷaja patently suggests that many new rāgas have been added to the stock.[40] Tulaja's work also proves that he is indebted to Sahaji I in many respects. Surprisingly, Tulaja had not openly acknowledged the source. He adds valuable hints in respect of Saṅcāras.[41] Sāṅgītasārāmṛta of Tulaja leaves Todī and Kalyāṇī mēḷas, but includes Vēḷāvali as a meḷa. King Sahaji I had ignored seventy-two melas and bases his lakṣaṇas only on twenty melas. King Sahaji's collection of Laksyas include Gītas of Venkatamakin couched in some well-known rāgas. Yet he has not popularised the seventy-two mēḷas. Perhaps, this patent omission strengthens the view that St. Tyāgarāja and Muttuswāmī Dīkṣitar popularised them.

The second half of the seventeenth century A.D. and the first half of the eighteenth century A.D. (post-Veṅkaṭamakin) witnessed an enormous increase of compositions in various rāgas. R. Ranga Rāmanujā Iyengar, the well-known musicologist gives 2116 Ārohaṇa-Avarohanas. He observes "Tyāgarāja used two-hundred and ten rāgas and Dīkṣitar a few less. Though the octave has only twelve notes, it is possible to permute and combine them deriving in the process more than forty-eight crores of all sorts. But only a few lend themselves for practical music worth the name...The table in the Appendix is an example product. Its only merit is it proves that patterns can be evolved."[42] P. Sāmbamūrthy, the eminent professor of music observes: "Geniuses conceive of melody first and rāgas of these melodies are analysed later... This has been the case of Tyāgarāja's compositions in rāgas not mentioned in earlier works... To know the advent of a new rāga, 'Modal shift of the tonic' could be taken into consideration as this may give an insight into the newcomer's basic structure (texture). Other tips provided are : (a) Ārohana-avarohana patterns under different meḷas; (b) Pratīmadhyama-Suddhamadama parallels; (c) Vilōma versions of the Ārohaṇa and Avarohaṇa of the same rāga; (d) Fusion of the Ārohana with the Vakra pattern of an Avarohana and vice versa and (e) Fusion of an avarohaṇa mūrchana with the avarohaṇa mūrçhana of a Janya rāga. These techniques are of a rigid and inflexible nature that their practical utility is open to doubt. If the new rāga does not have an aesthetic appeal, it may not stand the test of time. Rāga without aesthetic appeal could at best swell the quantity."[43]

Sāṁbamūrthy, recommends the extension of the Mēḷakarta scheme. His proposal is for having meḷas with Avarohaṇa of one meḷa and Ārohaṇa of another in addition to the seventy-two melas already known. Under this proposal, for instance Rāga Bairavī could be a meḷa. Ārohaṇa and Avarohana of Kanagāṅki, Ratnāṅki, Gānamūrt, etc., will form the first Çakra. (Kanaka-Çakra) of the seventy-two meḷas. The second (Ratna-Çakra) will have Ratnāṅki ārohaṇa and avarohaṇa of Kanagāṅki, Ratnāṅki, Gānamūrt etc. Reckoned this way there will be 72 × 72 or 5184 mēḷas. The first meḷa of Kanaka Çakra will be 'Kanakakanaka' (existing Kanagāṅki); the second mela 'Kanakarātna'; the third 'Kanakagāna' and so on. Sāmbamūrth's intention seems to be a desire to evolve a complete classification including the current rāgas and those that are likely to emerge later. Carnātic music is lakṣya-oriented (Lakṣyapradhāna or idealistic) and lakṣya is inspired by lakṣaṇa. Sāṁbamūrthi had made a cautious approach inasmuch as he realises that all the new meḷas cannot become rāgas. They are not likely to become aesthetic laden. They may gain the status of 'Alpa rāgas'. But Sāmbamūrthi had extended the meaning of meḷa. Yet, his proposals have not been widely accepted.

In the Tamil tradition 'sound' (Oḷi) is the primordial energy of the universe. Tolkāppiyam declares that the period of vibration of musical notes could be extended and measured with mathematical accuracy as in the fields of astronomy and astrology. Śaṅgam literature accepts 'Tiṇais', a tradition set by Tolkāppiyam.[44] Pans (Rāgas) and instruments of each of these regions (Tiṇai) bear individual characteristics. With the innovation of stringed instruments the idea of 'octave' is struck. To the Tamilians, the pentatonic scale had been the first to be known.[45] Every note of the Paṇ is a consonantal note to another note.[46] The septatonic scale was formed by filling the gaps of 'Ma' and 'Ni'. This is stated to be the Paṇ 'Śeṁpālai' identified with the Carnātic rāga 'Harikāmboti'.[47] Śeṁpālai is the fundamental scale of the Tamilians. With the Paṇ 'Mullai' as the base and by filling the gaps Harikāmboti, Vāçaspathi, Śaṅkarābharaṇam and Kalyāṇī (all Carnātic rāgas) could have come into existence. 'Mullai' is one of the physiographic divisions. (Tiṇai). This region is the abode of the shepherds. (Āyar) who use Veṅkulal. (Flute) Paripātal, the Śaṅgam anthology contains a reference to a 'Flute with five holes' as the first musical instrument to come into use.[48] Hence, it is suggested that five svaras (pentatonic) appeared first. *Śilappatikāram*, the Tamil epic written by Ilaṅkōaṭikaḷ endorses the statement of Paripātal.[49]

Tolkāppiyam refers to a variety of Pans.[50] Modes of producing sound and varieties of sound (Aśai) are referred to.[51] It also deals with metre and time-measure, emotion and rāga affiliations, prescriptions of the suitable times of the day or night for handling particular paṇs and grammar for maintaining rhythm.[52] Sound has the potential to reach the ear quickly and hence called 'Pā'.[53] Suitable syllables with power to create music, when properly handled form 'Aśai' and suitable combinations of 'Aśai' give rise to 'Śeer'.[54] Calculated vibration is 'Iśai'. Āśiriyappā, Veṅbā, Vançi and Kalippā are varieties of compositions. If chronologically arranged Āśiriyappā and Veṅbā take precedence.[55]

By an addition of five semi-tones to seven notes, the octave becomes complete with 'twelve notes' (Svarasthānas). They are known as the 'Twelve Kōvainilam'. By the process of the modal shift of the tonic at twelve points, the twelve scales are determined. The octave is divided into twenty-two 'Aḷakūs' (Sṛutis).[56] The seven notes are the seven 'Narampūs' and the five semi-tones are 'Antarakkol'. The twelve semi-tones are 'Nilattukkovai' and the octave is 'Mantilam'.[57] The order of the twelve notes is repeated in higher and lower octaves. Among the twelve, the flat notes are named 'Kuṛai-ñaraṁpūs' and the sharp ones are 'Niṛai-ñaraṁpūs'.[58] This basic framework of practical music in Tamil tradition remains unaltered and the tradition is traced to the 'Age of the Saṅgam' the earliest defined epoch of Tamil history.

Śilappatikāram is an informative treatise on music. It defines 'Svara' as that which satiates the desire for melody. 'Ñaraṁpu' is a term also used to describe the string in the musical instrument 'Yāl'...A 'note' springs when the string is plucked. The sound (note) is of two kinds namely 'Innā ñaraṁpu' and 'Iśai ñaraṁpu'. Other terms come into currency later.[59] The term 'Kōvai' must have been coined after fixation of the twelve svarasthānas (Kōvainilam).[60] Kōvai signifies the potential of the svaras to commingle with other svaras.[61] 'Kōvai' is the scale of measurement and this provides a derivative base for 'Kōl'.[62] The seven svaras are Kuṛal, Tuttam, Kaikkiḷai, Uḷai, Iḷi, Viḷari and Tāram.' Kuṛal and Iḷi are prakṛti svaras. The other five are Vikṛti svaras, each with two varieties making up the twelve. The twelve are called 'Paṇṇiru nilam' or 'Panniru nilai'.[63] 'Yeṛiya Kōvai', 'Iṛaṅkiya Kōvai' 'Niṛaikkōvai and Kuṛaikkōvai' are terms used to indicate flat and sharp notes. 'Mantilam' is a group of seven Kōvais or of twelve (7 + 5 = 12).[64] Saman, Melivu, Valivu and Mantilam are alternately known as Śennilai, Maṅtara, Tāra and Uççа maṇtilams.[65] Human voice is pliable in lower and higher maṇtilams to a limited extent. Such practical possibilities have been estimated. *Śilappatikāram* declares that in Melivu (four), Valivu (three) and Saman (seven) are the possibilities. The human voice could negotiate fourteen ñaraṁpūs (4 + 3 + 7).[66]

'Alaku' analogous to Sṛuti' is a sharp division of svara.[67] Śaṅgam literature as well as *Śilappatikāram* recognise twenty-two Aḷakus.[68] 'Aḷakus' are classified as (a) Nāṅkaḷukukkōvai, (b) Çatusṛuti, (c) Mūnraḷakukkōvai, (d) Tiśra Sṛuti, (e) Eraḷakukkōvai (Dvi Śṛuti).[69] The indispensability of the Tamburine (drone) is emphasized by *Śilappatikāram*. Paṇ (Rāga) means that which is done well in a manner to evoke aesthetic emotion (Meipātu). A 'scale' demands a characteristic glow to gain beauty. This depends on the sonant and consonant relationship of the notes (Iṇai and Kiḷai). *Śilappatikāram* makes mention of different paṇs.[70] Since deleting notes from the parent paṇs, only one set of the notes are excluded (Ma-Pa). If both the fourth and fifth notes are deleted, the resultant derivative will not be sharp. 'Pa' is the iṇai-ñarampu (Consonantal note) of 'Sa'. Inevitably one of them is indispensable to ensure stability and individuality.

Paṇs, thus derived have also been classified on the basis of the number of notes in the ascent as well as descent.[71] The classification of parent and derived paṇs is methodical. It had provided a substratum for many innovations. By adopting the modal shift of the tonic, 'Paṇṇiyāl' had been enriched.[72] Sempaṇ, provides innovation of parent paṇs by adoption of modal shift of the tonic. References in *Śilappatikāram* show that the results have been consolidated.

Aṭiyārkkunallār, the commentator of *Śilappatikāram* lists seven ñarampūs of Śempālai.[73] 'Śempālai' is equated with Śaṅkarābharaṇam (of the Carnātic system) by Abrahām Paṇḍitar; and with Harikāmboti by Vipulānantar and S. Ramanatan. Vi. Pa. Ka. Sundaram affirms that Śempālai is the basic as identified by Arumpatauraiyar, Aṭiyārkkunallār, Iḷaṅko Aṭikaḷ, Pañçamarapu of Arivāṇar and Nikaṇṭūs.[74]

Appropriate pans for all the Tiṇais (physiographic divisions) are mentioned. Scholars identify the 'Ñāṛperumpaṇs'; but they sharply differ while pairing individual pans with Tiṇais.[75] Codes set by *Śilappatikāram* in this regard are similar to those set by Pañçamarapu.[76] Śevvaḷippālai, Arumpālai and Merśempālai are added to the original ones (Perumpālais) and thus the total of seven is made up. (Yeḷ Perumpālais) Arumpālai belongs to the barren tract (Pālai).

'Gṛhabehdam' (Gṛhasvarabhedam) is the process of finding a new scale by the shift of the tonic note in a basic scale.[77] The scale to which the process is applied is taken as the base. Taking each 'note' of the basic scale as the tonic (Ādhāra Ṣaḍjam) and playing the self same notes of the original scale, new scales came to light. There is a redistribution of intervals because of the shift in Āhdāra Ṣaḍja, Saṅgam anthologies make a reference to the process as

'Paṇ peyartal' (Pālai paṇṇal).[78] *Śilappatikāram* calls it as 'Paṇ peyartal'.[79]

'Gamaka' is another important concept which finds no mention in Bharata's Nāṭyaśāstra.[80] Yet usage of 'Gamaka' had gained significance and importance. In the Alaṅkāra section we come across with the term 'Kaṁpa' (Reçita, Kuhara, Kaṁpita). It is related to the Tāra, Madhya and Maṅdra stānas. This gains greater attention and emphasis at the hands of Mataṅga. Some scholars suggest 'Kala' as the distinguished feature in view of 'Stāna'. Abhinavagupta refers to the existence of both the views. He also suggests that 'Kala' in Alaṅkāra is to be identified with 'Sruti'. He identifies 'Kampa' with 'Svarita' (Three Sruti intervals) Nānyadeva's *Bharatabhāṣya* and Somesvara's *Mānasōllāsa* (11th century A.D.) mention seven varieties of Gamaka. Later texts (since A.D. 13th century) follow *Saṅgītaratnākaram* of Śāraṅgadeva. Ratnākaram defines Gamaka, lists and describes fifteen varieties.

The Dagara tradition of Hindustānī Drupad accepts ten svaralakṣaṇas of which Gamaka is one.[81] In Khyāl, Gamaka stands for the extra breath force in ālāpa or tāna. From the eighteenth century A.D., a distinct oral tradition is noticeable. This tradition recognises the 'Daśavita gamakas'.[82] Literary expression is found in (a) Saṅgītasāra saṅgrahaṃu (Telugu edition, A.D. 1800), (b) Mahābharāta cūḍāmaṇi (Chapter IV), (c) Saṅgītarāgameḷalakṣaṇam (Tamil), (d) Vīṇālakṣaṇam of Paramesvara (Gaekwad Oriental Series, Baroda, n.d.), (e) Saṅgitasampradāya Pradarśini of Subbarāma Dīkṣitar (1904-05). Subbarāma Dīkṣitar makes an attempt to consolidate ten Gamakas, and since then we hear of ten or fifteen Gamakas.

'Uḷḷōśai' is the equivalent of 'Gamaka' in the Tamil tradition. It is a collective term referring to jerks, graces, ornamentations and embellishments. They result from the quiver of notes or manipulation of notes in a spicey way to claim attention of the listener. It is an integral part of the music and an essential part of the melodic structure. They lend glamour (colour) to the music and are comparable with the phenomenon of harmony of the Western system of music. Continuity in Carnātic music depends on the successful handling of the Gamakas. They help in the fixation of the melodic content of the rāga handled and literally form the backbone of the rāgas. Use of Gamakas represent the particular quality of an individual artiste's music. Instrumentalists use techniques of their own in handling Gamakas.[83]

Abundant references to Uḷḷōśai are found in the Tamil epic *Śilappatikāram.*[84] 'Vārtal, Vaṭittuṭal, Untal, Melivu, Melivin untal, Teruttal, Aḷḷal and Pattākai' are the terms mentioned in the epic.[85] Piṅgala Nikhaṇtu enumerates six Uḷḷōśais and Śēndan Divākaram restates them.[86]

The classification of Pālai is dependent on Śṛuti.[87] Kōvai split in halves and quarters (Pāya) has potential to widen the canvas. Fractions into one, half, quarter and one by eight are spoken of as four pāyās. (Pāyam nāṅkum).[88] Reference to one hundred and three paṇs are found scattered. Piṅgaḷa Nikhaṇṭu gives the names of Paṇs, but there are no indications to fix the svaras of each paṇ.

Rules relating to the lakṣaṇa and elaboration of rāgas have not been scrupulously followed. Nowhere had it been possible to locate precedence extended practice in conformity with original norms. It is obvious that the usage of today becomes the grammar of tomorrow. It is however remarkable that when the freedom in the matter of rendering the rāgas is almost in some respects unlimited, their character and complexion had changed very little during the past six centuries. At present, a rāga is described with reference to its appropriate méla, ārohaṇa and avarohaṇa, special or extra noṭe taken by it, characteristic prayōgas (application) and comprehensive saṅgatīs. It is in the ālāpa (elaboration) of a rāga by competent artistes or in the songs of master composers can we hope to get a full picture.

REFERENCES

1. Lakṣaṇa Graṅtha: A treatise which deals with the principles. (Lakṣaṇas). 'Lakṣyate anena iti lakṣaṇam'.
2. Āsvālayana Śrauta sūtra:

   Ekaśṛutyam: "Ekaśṛuti satatam bhūyāt :

   Para: Sannikarṣa Saṅgītaratnākara: Ārçika: Ekasvarigānam.
3. T.V. Kuppuswami: *Carnatic Music and the Tamils,* p. 2, fn. 56.
4. Later Saṅgīta literature. (Paper read at the Madras Music Conference, 1931). Also refer Appendix.
5. They are 1, 9/8, 6/5, 4/3, 3/2, 27/16, 8/5, 2. The intervals are 9/8, 6/15, 10/9, 9/6, 9/8, 16/15, 10/9. Ref: Ahōbala: Saṅgītapārijāta.

6. They take the values 256/243, 25/24 or 81/80 as applicable. In cyclic cents these intervals have the values 90, 70, 22.
7. Ratio value of these twelve notes with reference to the basic note are 7, 10/9, 9/8, 6/5, 5/4, 4/3, 40/27, 3/2, 5/3, 27/16, 9/5, 15/8, 2.
8. H.H. Popely, *The Music of India,* New Delhi, 1966.
9. Yannōktam Baratātibhi: tatāsmābhi: nirūpayate.

   (Bṛhaddesī, Trivandrum Sanskrit Series, No. XCIV)

   Dr. Raghavan places Mataṅga the author of Bṛhaddeśī in the ninth century A.D. (Bulletin of the Saṅgīta Nātaka Academy. No. 5) P.V. Kane places Mataṅga in A.D. 750.
10. Infra: Same chapter.
11. Rāga 'Kalyāṇī' of the sixty-fifth mela is one such in current usage. It finds no mention in works like Makaraṅtam and Ratnākaram. Loçāna makes mention of it in Rāgataraṅgiṇi and calls it Yemen (Émen).
12. Mataṅga: Bṛhaddeśī, *op. cit.,* pp. 81-140.
13. The legend is that Lord Śiva has five heads which produced one rāga each and Pārvatī added one to them and the six 'Purusa-rāgas' came into vogue. Each of these rāgas has five 'Rāginis'. By the admixture of the Rāginis with the Puruṣa rāgas, five Janya rāgas were born to each rāgini.
14. Puṇḍarīka Viṭṭala (A.D. 1590) The Bikanir catalogue describes three works of Viṭṭala, namely *Rāgamāla, Rāgamañjari,* and *Sadrāgaçaṅdrodaya.* He lived in the court of Burhan Khān (A.D. 1370 to 1600), a Muslim king at Ānaṅdavalli in Kāndesh in the south. His *Rāgamañjari* praises Akbar "under whom the princes of Kaççabi vamśa (Mādhava Simha and Mānava Simha) served." In *Rāgamañjari,* Viṭṭala gives fifteen new 'Parasiddarāgas' as a consequence of which Meḷapaddati gains importance.
15. Rāmamātya is the contemporary of Rāmarāga of Vijayanagar. M.S. Rāmaswāmī Iyer of the Annamalai University, Tamil Nadu had edited and published the work 'Svarameḷakalānidī'. Three editions of the work are available. (1) An old south-Indian edition, (2) A Marāthi edition with notes by Bhathtkande and (3) Annamalai University series authored by M.S. Rāmaswāmī Iyer. Similarities are noticed between Samagāmana Saptaka (In vogue during Ramamātyar's time) and Karaharapriya meḷa of the Carnatic style. (Kafithāt).

   Rāmamātya had clear ideas about Vīṇā and its play. (Stringed instrument) This is evidenced by the Chapter on 'Vīṇā Prakaraṇa' of the work. The Vīṇā he used was Rudra Vīṇā. Three varieties are mentioned: Śudda meḷa, Madhyameḷa and Acyuta Rājendra meḷa. Śudda mēḷa Vīṇā has six frets, four metal strings and three strings on the sides. In the chapter on Meḷaprakaraṇa, for the first time he used the term 'Meḷa' in the sense of 'Genus'. He mentions twenty melas and their svaras: Mukāri, Mālawagauḷa, Śrī Rāga, Sārangā nāṭa, Hiṅdōla, Śuddarāmakriya,

Dēśākṣi, Kannada gauḷa, Śudda-nāttai, Āhiri, Nādanāmakriya, Hejjuji, Sāmavarāḷi, Rēvagupti, Sāmanta, Kāmbōji. His concept of the technique of Madyameḷa Vīṇā is a milestone in the history of Rāga development in the Carnātic system of music.

16. "Tatra laksmanurōtēna gāndharvam sampryukyatē.

 Yatra lakṣya arityāgē pratyavāyōna vidyate

 Tasmāt lakśyapradhānam tannōtu lakṣyaprathānēkam

 Paritīyagē asya lakṣyasya ranjanam naiva jāyaté

 Tasmāt lakṣyapradhāna gānam lokē pravartatē.

 (Svaramēḷakalanidhi, Annāmalai edn. p. 14).

17. Veṅkaṭamakin. (A.D. 1620) states that Rāmamātya could not understand what a shepherd would.

 "Tata hi vimśatīrmēḷanakō Rāmō vimūdamati:

 (Çaturdaṇḍiprakāśika, IV. 167)

 "Satyam vinoksayasē Rāma Rāma-Sētum gatōpi vā Rāmō çatramā paśupālopi budhyaté".

18. He proclaims that Śudda meḷa (Mukhāri) is just the 'Ṣaḍji mūrça' of 'Ṣaḍjagrāma' of Bharata and Sāmgadeva. This seems to be an error. This indicates the influence of Rāmamātya who named it Mukhāri (Kanakānki at present) having all the seven Śudda notes. 'Śudda scale' of Bharata is like Karaharapriya of the present day. Śudda-scale of Rāmamātya differs in four notes (Ri, Ga, Da and Ni) from that of Bharata while Sa, Ma, and Pa are common to both. Sōmanāta author of Rāgavibōdha commits an identical error. Musical terminology and nomenclature have changed by A.D. 1680, when Veṅkaṭamakin wrote.

19. As to the possible objection of the 'Sama' note playing in dual role of Riṣaba and Gāṇdhāra/ Dhaivata and Niṣāda: Veṅkaṭamakin gives the analogy of four brothers A, B, C and D. 'A' has the character of only the younger brother and 'D' that of the elder brother. But 'B' is an elder brother to 'A' and younger to 'C' and 'D'. 'C' is an elder brother to 'A' and 'B' and the younger to 'D'. In effect 'B' and 'C' take their names relative to the 'Notes' with which they combine.

20. "Prasidda: punaryetēṣu mela: katācitē vā hi

 Dṛśyantē na tu sarvē api tēna kalpanam vṛtā

 Kalpanā gaura yayiti-çetitamuçyatē

 Ananta: Kalu dēśāstat dēśāstapi mānava:

 Tēṣu Saṅgītikairucca vaça Saṅgīta kovidai:

 Yē Kalpayiṣyamānaśça kalpayamānaśça kalpita : II.

21. Veṅkatamakin seems to enjoy his own classification when he exclaims "All my efforts would be in vain if any one can make more or less than seventy-two *melas* out of the twelve 'notes'. Even Lord Śiva will not dare do so."

22. *Ārohana* and *Avarohana* are to be taken into consideration to check that all the svaras of the scale are present. 'Kanakāmbari' nomenclature given in the appendix of Çaturdaṇḍiprakāśika (Music Academy, Madras) is to be placed at a chronologically much later period.

23. All the notes of the mela are present in both Ārohaṇa and Avarohaṇa. 'Saṅgīta Saṅgrahamu' is an anonymous work noticed in the catalogue of the MSS in Mysore and Coorg. Oppert also makes mention of the work. (Conjeevaram (Kāñcīpuram) Volume I, 1052).

24. A casual reference to the work is made in Çaturdaṇḍiprakāśika. Name of the author and other details are unknown. With twenty-four Sṛtis as twenty-four *svarastānas*, the author evolves a scheme of melās. His scheme includes 4624 meḷas. His scheme remains a theoretical postulate.

25. For example, 'Dheera' was prefixed to Śaṅkarābharaṇam and the scale is named 'Dheera Śaṅkarābharaṇam'.

    T.V. Kuppuswami : *Carnatic Music and the Tamils,* Chapter X, pp. 200-202.

26. (1) Indu (2) Netra (3) Agni (4) Vedas (5) Bāṇa (6) Ṛtus (7) Ṛṣis (8) Vasus (9) Brahma (10) Diśi (11) Rudra and (12) Ādityas.

27. Vādī is compared to the king, Samvādī to the minister, Anuvādī to the servant and Vivādī to the enemy. The king has to destroy the enemies and Vivādī form is to be destroyed if the Rāga is to gain Rakti.

    "Vivādī Vādī Samvādī bhinna: syurānuvādina:
    Caturvita svarēṣvēṣu vādirājaprakeertayate
    Samvāritvaanuśāritvadasyamātyō vidheeyetē
    Vivādivipreetāt vat dheerairaktōripupama:
    Śivarūpamardanē hi syāt ragyām lōke prakāśānām
    Nrpamatyānusarit Vādānuvādi tu bridyavat II

    Some compositions of St. Tyāgarāja (Tiruvaiyāru) are in Vivādī rāgas. Out of six hundred and seventy-five of the compositions, just forty-five are in Vivādī mélas—out of which fourteen are in the rāga Varāḷi.

28. The scheme of seventy-two mēḷas in Carnātic music, *Journal of the Music Academy,* Vol. XI, Madras, pp. 80-86.

29. A Telugu manuscript bearing the title 'Saṅgītaśāstrasaṅkṣepa' came into circulation very late after its discovery at the Adayar Manuscript Library by K.V. Rāmachandran. This work is authored by Gōvinda and its date remains a speculation. It was deemed that this work formed the basis of Tyāgarāja's music. C.R. Srinivasa Iyengar felt that this work must be placed chronologically earlier to Veṅkatamakin. The net result of the discovery of the work is the generation of a controversy about the compositions of Tyāgarāja and Muttuswāmī Dīkṣitar.

30. References : 1. Rāgalakṣaṇa (appended to Çaturdaṇḍi prakāśika of Veṅkaṭamakin. Music Academy edition) 2. Catvārivimśat śata-rāga nirūpaṇa (B.S. Suktanakar, Aryabushan Press, Bombay) 3. Rāgalakṣaṇa (B.S. Suktanakar, Aryabushan Press, Bombay).

31. The ancient Sudda-scale was 'Śrī-rāga' (modern Karaharapriya. 22nd mēḷa of Veṅkatamakin), while the Hindustānī is the Niṣād mūrçana of the same scale Vēlāvali or Bilāval which is analogous to Śaṅkarābharanam, the 29th mela of Veṅkaṭamakin. Śrī Rāga scale is the Śuddasvara Saptaka of Śārṅgadeva. Lōçana, Ahōbala, Hṛudaya-nārāyaṇa and Śrīnivāsa. The modern Hindustānī scale is the Bilāval, the corrupt form of Vélāvaḷi of Śārṅgadēva who used it for naming the Niṣādi Jāti.

32. Sadrāga Caṅdrōdaya. (B.S. Suktanakar, Nirnayasagar Press, Bombay, 1912).

33. Çatura kallināta's commentary is called 'Kalānidhi'. (Ānaṅdāśramam Series). Reference is found under the caption 'Adhunaprasidha rāgas'. (p. 217). Kallināta's commentary is the most popular.

"Nāṭṭa dévakree prabūtiṣu riṣabha dhaivatayō: antaré kākaḷyātima I

Sṛtidvayaknamaṇéna pratyékam paṅcasṛtitā"

(Applies to Nāta and Dévakriya rāgas).

34. Daṣakūṭas: T.V. Kuppuswami: *Carnātic Music and the Tamils,* Chapters VIII-X.

35. *Kuta tānas*: A series of svaras arranged without any sequence or order.

36. 'Keçit desityā peerita' (Prasidda grāma Rāgādhyāya).

37. Saṅgītamakaraṅda is assigned to the eleventh centrury A.D. and the author is Nārada. In respect of chronology, opinions differ. Ninety-three different rāgas are enumerated in the chapter on Rāgas. Rāgas are classified into Purusa (male) and Stree (female) and Putra (neuter) rāgas. He also speaks of Muktāṅga-Kaṁpita (All svaras rendered into Gamaga). Ardha Kampita (notes rendered with Gamakas and Kampa vihīna (without Gamakas).

38. It seems to continue in the same méḷa in the Hindustānī system. (Vélāvala).

39. Gāndhāra Pançama, Bhinna pançama, Mēgharaṅçani (Vēgaraṅçani), Nāga Gāndāri, Madyamagrāma (Udaya), Ravicandrika are names found in the Saṅgītaratnakāram.

Kāpi, Husseini, Balahamsa, Gauda Malhar, (Tilapa) Julāva, Bilsāni, Lalita Pancamam have been incorporated by king Tuḷaja. Their origin could be traced to the Hindustānī system. Some names are native in origin. Husseini, Sahāna, Aṭāna, Bilahari Kānada, Kāmaja, Kāpi, Jenjūti, Durbār, Dvijāvanti (Jujavanti), Navarōz, Nāyaki, Pūrvi Kalyānī, Paras Balahamsa, Bégaḍa, Béhāg, Māñji, Yedukula-Kāmbōji, Yamunā Kalyāṇī. Bairava, Gaudamalhār, Jaṅgaḷa, Julāv Vrindāvāni, Déśi Tōdé Syāma, Manjarī Dilīpika, Kālagaḍa, etc. are as such.

Rāgas not traceable before the time of Tuḷaja are Abhōgi, Keervāni, Garudadvani, Cakravākam, Janaraṅjanī, Saṅtāna mañjarī, Malayamārutam, Śāramati, Mañjarī Dévamṛta varṣiṇi, Çittarañjani, etc.

40. Laksanas given by Sahāji are available in ten manuscripts.
Tanjāvūr Mannar Serfoji, Saraswatimahal Library:
B. No. 11548 to 11555, 1620 and 1621.
41. R. Rengaramanuja Iyengar: History of South Indian-(Carnātic) music-from Vedic times to the present. (Sabarmati, Sait Colony, Madras, 1972)
Appendix IV, Mēḷa-Janya rāga Table, pp. XXXII-CXXIX
He adds : The following Table contains anomalies and inconsistencies that has to be resolved in the light of current traditions.
B. Suṅdaram: Pālai Yāl (Tamil). Suṅdaram provides a list of more than three thousand scales.
42. P. Sāmbamurthi : (1) Rāga Classification in Indian Music (Lecture in Indian Music, Queen Mary's College, Madras, 1930).
(2) The origin of some rāgas, (*op. cit.,* J.M.A XVI, 1945).
43. Tolkāppiyam: Eluttu Atikāram; Akaṭṭiṇai. 18.
44. K. Śivathambi : *Tinaikkōtpātin Samūka Adippataikaḷ.* (Tamil Arōici (ed.) N. Vanamamalai, July, 1971).
45. Mullaippaṇ is the first pentatonic scale used in Tamil music. This is identified as a Rāga.
46. V. Pa. Ka. Suṅdaram: Development of a Rāgam. Heritage of the Tamils, Art & Architecture (ed) S.V. Subramanian and A.N. Perumal. Institute of International Tamil Studies, Madras, 1980, p. 72.
47. Mullaippaṇ: Sa, ri, ga, pa, da, sa (DECAC). Śeṁpālai: Sa, ri, ga, ma, pa, da, ni, sa.
48. Paripāṭal: 8: 22-23.
H.H. Popely (The Music of India, Y.M.C.A., New Delhi, 1966.)
49. Śilappatikāram (4) Aṅtima 15.
50. Śeyyuḷ: 80-81.
51. Piṛappiyal: Sūtras 3, 5, 6, 15, 16, Śeyyuḷ 80-83, Nūnmarapu 3.33.
52. Śeyyuḷ 95, Mei. 10.
Nūṛpā: Kārum malayum mullaikkuriya; mutal vaḷi pāyinum yāppinam Çitayum, vallōn puṇara vāram pōnré.
53. Pā=Potential to spread. Hence Pāṭṭu=Song.
54. *Tolkāppiyam*: Śeyyuḷ 10.
55. *Ibid:* Śeyyuḷ 107.
56. Alakū—the sharpest audible fraction of a quartertone or semi-tone.
57. Etymological meaning of Maṇtilam is 'that which hovers round'. 'Sa' and 'Pa' are fixed. The remaining five (ri, ga, ma, da, ni) each receives four Alakūs. 5 x 4 = 20. 20 + 2 = 22.
58. *Ñaṛampu, Kōvai, Tantri* and *Kōl* are mentioned in *Piṅgaḷa Nikaṇdu*, the grammar.

59. Śilappatikāram: (3) Araṅkēṟṟu (73) commentary Atiyārkkunallār.
60. Śilappatikāram: Vénir (8) 31-32.
61. Śilappatikāram: Vénir Commentary on L.27.
62. Śilappatikāram: 17, 13-8: 9:10.
63. Śilappatikāram: 17, Aōiciyar Kuravai. L3 Commentary.
64. Śilappatikāram: *Ibid.*
65. Śilappatikāram: 3. Araṅkērrukkātai. 93.
66. Araṅkērrukkāṭai: 70, Veṅrikkūttu 31, 32, 8.
67. Mantilam is divided (Stāyi) into seven ñarampūs (svaras). It again gets split into twelve half-*Kōvais*. This twelve again could be split into twenty-two units which are not however, equal. Yet, if properly handled it produces melody. Paṇs (Rāgas) of different shades are born. Western system recognises 'Equal divisions' and gives the name 'Equal temperament'. Instruments like organ, harmonium, etc., are structured on this principle. This is also known by the name of 'Just intonation'.
68. Abraham Paṇḍitar: Karṇāmṛta Sāgaram (Tanjore 1917) refers to 24, 32 and 48 *Alakūs.*
69. V.Pa.Ka. Sundaram: Paḷamtamiḷ Ilakkiyattil Iśai Iyal *op. cit.*, pp. 70-80.

    Vipulānandar made the first attempt and S. Ramanathan followed K. Kothandapaniar. (Ref: Paḷamtamiḷ Iśai. S.S.N. Veḷiyeedu 1959) Sundaram endorses the view.
70. Śilappatikāram: 8. *Vēnir Kātai.* L.35. The commentary mentions *Yāḷ, Pālai, Arakkam, Iśai.* Four varieties of Paṇ are: 1. Perumpaṇ (Sampūrnam Septatonic 7=7), (2) Paṇṇital (Shāḍavam. Septa-tonic 6 = 6), (3) Tiram (Auḍavam. Hepta-tonic 5+5), 4. Tirāttiram (Çaturtam. Quadruple tonic 4+4).
71. Paṇ-paṇ (Sexta-tonic 7+7); Paṇpaṇṇiyāl (Sexta-septa tonic 7+6); Paṇtiram (Sexta penta tonic 7+5); Paṇ tirāttiram (Sexta quadruple tonic 7+4); Paṇṇiyāl paṇ (Septa-sexta tonic 6+7); Paṇṇiyal paṇṇiyāl (Septa-septa tonic 6+6); Paṇṇiyāl tiram (Septa-penta tonic 6+5); Paṇṇiyāl Tirattiram (Septa Quadruple tonic 6+4); Tiram Paṇ (Septa-penta tonic 7+5); Tiram Paṇṇiyāl (Penta-septa tonic 5+6); Tiram-tiram (Penta-penta tonic); Tirat-tirattiram (Penta Quadruple tonic).
72. 'Viḷari' is an example.
73. Śilappatikāram: 17. Aōiçiyar Kuravai. Commentary on L.13.
74. Paḷam Tamil ilakkiyattil Iśai-iyal., *op. cit.*, pp. 108-22.
75. Tolkāppiyam suggests Mullai Yāḷ (Mullaipperumpaṇ) Kuṟiñçi Yāḷ (Kuṟiñçipperumpaṇ) Maruta Yāḷ (Marutapperumpaṇ), Neital Yāḷ (Neital Perumpaṇ), Tolkāppiyam: Śeyyūl. 95, Mei 10, Nūṟpa 3:33 Yāḷ is a stringed instrument. Each region has one as Mullai Yāḷ, Kuṟiñçi Yāḷ; Maruta Yāḷ; and Neital Yaḷ. In the present context it refers to 'Perumpaṇ' with seven 'Ñarampūs'.

76. Pañçamarapu: Venbā "Tarattu Ulai tōnṛa Iḷiyil Pirakka neital Yāl."

77. 'Gṛhabhēdam'— 'Gṛhasvara bhēdam' is the process of finding a new scale by the shift of the tonic-note in a basic scale. Musicologists of India and Arabia, Greece and Rome know this process as 'Modal shift of the tonic'.

78. Patiṛṛuppattu: 65:14 (Pāval kaival pānar).

79. Śilappatikāram: 7. *Kānal vari.* L.47. V.Pa. Ka. Sundaram: *Paḻam Tamil Ilakkiyattil Iśai Iyal, op., cit.*, pp. 163-80.

80. A single text-variant refers to it. Competent scholars consider this reference as an interpolation.

81. In poetics 'Lakṣaṇa' is parallel to 'Alankāra' (a) Akāra (b) Dagra (c) Dṛva (d) Muraṇa (e) Kampita (f) Āṅdoḷikā (g) Gamaka (h) Hudaka (i) Spurte.

82. Muttuswāmī Dīkṣitar's composition 'Meenākṣi' in the rāga 'Pūrvikalyāṇī'

83. (a) 'Kampita' (long and short) (b) Spurita (c) Bṛge (d) Jāru (e) Āhata (f) Ōrivi (g) Katri (h) Nokku (i) Tṛipuççа.

84. Ērattal (Doubling of notes)-(Ss, Ri-ri,Gg, Mm)

Śilambal (Closed mouth singing) Ārōśai (gliding through few notes up Srgm); *Amarōśai* (Gliding through some notes down mgrs); Ūñçal (Singing of a note to impinge on either range (pmpd): *Maharam viraval* (Humming); hopping to another note and returning to a particular note (Sa-ma, sa-pa; sa-dha) *Muraḷvu* (playing one of the notes softly); *Naraḷvu* (playing one of the notes pretty long (Ma-pa); *Teḷivu* (playing one of the notes briefly and forcefully); *Vilaivu* (returning or resting on a note (Ma, Pa, Dha); *Nuṇukkam* (single note begins with stress and slowly wanes); *Kaḷittal* (Jumping on a note from a note—Sa, ga, ri, ma, ga, ri); *Kampalai* (tremulous shaking of notes); *Kōdanai* (gliding on finger board); *Kodu* (join one note with another).

85. Kānalvari: 12-16; 3:9; 60, 3:63.

86. Piṅgaḷa Nikaṇṭu: 1, 36, 1441 *Muraḷvu, Tāḷvi, Gyēlvi Vilaivu, Nuṇukkam, Kampalai,* (Nadukkam), *Aṭukkal* and *Makaraviśai* (Iḷimiśai). *Divākaram* speaks of *Vilaivu* as Uḷai.

87. Śilappatikāram: 13, 17. Commentary.

88. Abraham Panditar: *Karṇāmṛta Sāgaram, op. cit.*, pp. 871, 933, 1022, and 1149.

3
Canons

Ronald Barthes in a fine text on Beethoven wrote "To listen to music in the network of composition is to rewrite it ; to put music into operation to draw it towards the unknown praxis."[1] In composition, music emerges as a relation to the body and the transcendence. A composition is a 'labour on sounds in search of thoughts'. It ensures the voice, those rhythms and sounds which are the supreme mode of relation. Composition needs its own technology as a basis for support as a new form of value. According to Cage, "Music is not to be produced in a temple, not in a hall nor at home but 'everywhere'. It is to be produced 'everywhere' it is possible to produce it in whatever way it is wished by anyone who wants to enjoy it. The composer should give up the desire to control sound, clear his mind of music and set about discovering means to let sound to be themselves rather than vehicles for man-made theories or expressions for human sentiments."[2] As against this conception Claude Levy Strauss feels that "it is difficult to concede that there exists in each person the potential for musical creation". He writes "Theoretically, if not in fact, any adequately educated man could write poems good or bad, whereas musical invention depends on special talents, which can be developed only where they are innate."[3]

In the western system musical forms developed on rhythm and harmonious components. Indian musical forms are melody oriented. Musical forms admit varieties of tonal structure (concrete) projecting musical culture of the 'country composition'—"A labour on sounds without a grammar, without a directing thought, a pretext for festival in search of thoughts—" it is not a central network. Compositions give voice to the feeling that rhythm and sound are the supreme mode of relation between the bodies once the screens of the symbolic usage and exchange are shattered. Evidently, in the western system, music seems to have been directly transacted by desires and drives—had always had one subject—the body which it offers a complete journey through pleasure, with a beginning and an end.,

Indian music (particularly Carnātic) is devotional. Being 'sacred' it led to the emergence of devotional musical forms. Such forms admit of variety and beauty. Each variety has a charm of its own and forms the link of an ordained musical chain. Varieties of composition (musical forms) are categorised as 'Kalpita' and 'Manōdharma' and also as 'Nibadda' and 'Anibadda'. Those which are premeditated and set to music (tuned) are treated as 'Kalpita Saṅgīta'. Compositions that spring forth spontaneously are treated as 'Manōdharma Saṅgīta'. Improvisations of a performer too come under this category. They are characterised by originality and talent. 'Kalpita' compositions are often intended to lead the prospective composer or performer along the right path. 'Kalpita Saṅgīta' must have come earlier. It is to be taken as the 'guardian of tradition'.

The term 'tradition' in the present context has a special connotation. Conservatism turns into historicism the moment the survival into the currency of things past are subjected to scrutiny. This scrutiny leads to the conviction or feeling that past things form an essential part of the present precisely in being from the past and because of some substances within them that have withstood all changes. Historical faculty that analyses works on music in the context of their time of origin, should be taken virtually intact into AESTHETIC EXPERIENCE; the two should not be kept apart by a rigid compartmentalisation of art into its AESTHETIC and DOCUMENTARY aspects. Awareness of the past is not incompatible with the aesthetic present. On the contrary, it can be a component part of the present. The historicist firmly believes that what a work has to say about the age in which it was written belongs at once and at the same time to the past and the present; not because works are timeless, but because past and present form an indissoluble alloy. The past is what has survived from the past and hence is part and parcel of the present. The works that have extended from earlier periods into our own age do not come solitary and sequestered. They bring their own time— *A TEMPS PERDU*— along with them. The traditionalist clings to a metaphysics of timeless beauty in the abstract. The conservative clings to the belief that behind the various manifestations of a thing, there lies an unchanging and inviolable substance. The historicist enjoys past things for being past in the form of a recollection that figures as an essential feature of the present moment. The remote is perceived as such, but experienced as near, the foreign is recognised as alien, yet felt to be familiar. The ultimate message of historicism is a *TWISTED AESTHETIC PARADOX*. In reviewing the relationship between 'Kalpita' and 'Manōdharma Saṅgīta' such a paradox is latent.

Aestheticising the history and historicising the aesthetics are the two sides of the same coin. The meaning of the art bears the stamp of history more and more. In extreme cases it appears to be historical through and through. This gives rise to the tendency to view history as a broad panorama to be gazed upon in aesthetic contemplation. The distinction between democratic and documentary sides of music is not uncompromising. It is equally possible to trace the emancipation of art towards aesthetic autonomy. Historical and aesthetic thoughts belong to the same current in the 'history of ideas'.

The poetic element of music is that which qualifies music as an art-form. This element is sought in the originality with which a composer expresses his own thought and being. He tries to prove himself equal to the paradoxical task of making us sense the 'indescribable and ineffable'. The question of how we understand a composer, retains its urgency in the aesthetics and history of music. Art-music and other varieties of the art call for 'personal expression'. This demand continues to exercise its uncontested supremacy in the art of composing and in performing. While estimating the value of a composition we are unable to know where we should draw the bounds within which we may criticise the past view in terms of its own age without running the risk of being accused of anachronism and wilfulness. Since effecting a value judgement it becomes necessary to make aesthetic distinctions. For making aesthetic distinctions the following tools help: (a) Pre-existent canon passed down by tradition. (Structural history). The nature of and the reasons for the formation of the canons can be scrutinised. (b) Categories, criteria and modes of thought of the composers. These may be contrasted with each other and arranged methodically. (c) Aesthetic norms cognisable in compositions belonging to different periods of time. This would mean that the investigation turns into a 'tradition criticism project'. The conception of novelty as an aesthetic criterion contains historical elements. Careful valuation demands that aesthetic value-judgement should not fall a victim to an objective historical one. Music history cannot be freed from aesthetics.

Tamil Nadu (where Carnātic music is popular) true to its romantic heritage allowed national factors in culture and perhaps overrated them. In line with 'romantic conservatism' it exploited the apparently immutable, constant and eternal principles of cultural development against progressive reformist and sometimes revolutionary political tendencies. Everything that seemed indigenous and seemed to accord with native culture, everything which was apparently arbitrarily created and which could not be changed overnight was felt to be useful, wholesome and fruitful. Carnātic music in operation remains Carnātic music, just as the Tamils remain Tamils.[5]

The Tamil language has the unique distinction of being spoken of as 'Muttamiḷ':— Iyal (literary), Iśai (music) and Nāṭakam (drama). There are copious references to music in the Tamil anthologies belonging to the pre-Christian era.[6] The well-known Tamil epic Śilappatikāram is hailed as 'Muttamiḷ Kāppiyam' that is a poetic work dealing with triple aspects—literary, musical and dramatic. Tolkāppiyam is the oldest extant literary work in Tamil. Its influence is traceable in all the periods of Tamil literary history in various degrees. In the 'Śeyyuḷ Iyal of Tolkāppiyam' we find references to thirty varieties of compositions.[7] Post-Tolkāppiyam musicologists follow the codes faithfully. Verses in the Śaṅgam anthologies are in the *Akaval* metre, perhaps the simplest. In pre-Tolkāppiyam age the *Kali* metre seems to have been popular. Composing in Kali metre demands some element of melody injected into the structure. Perhaps the reasons for the Śaṅgam poets for adopting *Akaval* is their desire for making their compositions intelligible to the uninitiated. *Tiruvalluvar,* author of the well known *Tirukkuṛal* follows Tolkāppiyam. But he has made a novel approach to *'Śeyyuḷiyal'*.[8] Like the poets of the *Saṅgam* age, Tiruvaḷḷuvar adopted a simple and short format in order to make it easily understandable.

Legends make us believe that Akattiyar wrote a treatise covering all the three divisions—*Iyal, Iśai* and Nāṭakam and that there was a treatise 'Baratam'. All these have been irretrievably lost. It was Saint Tirugñānasambandar who restored Tamil music to ancient glory.[9] His hymns are employed in worship in the temples of Tamil Nadu. A young woman of Tirukkāttāmpuliyūr, the birthplace of Tirunīlakaṇṭha Yālpāṇar set tunes to *Tevāram* hymns.[10] The Çōḷa monarch Kulōttuṅga I was himself a fine composer and his queen Yēḷiśai Vallapi (expert in handling the seven notes) used to sing his compositions.

The ninth book in the Śaiva Canon (series) is called 'Tiruviśaippā' (book of musical sayings). Atiyārkkunallār, the well known commentator elaborates the theory of music in his commentary on Śilappatikāram. This elaboration perhaps inspired the author of Tiruppukaḷ namely Aruṇagirināthar. The three 'Karuvai Antātis' of Varaguṇa Pāṇḍyan (later medieval period), various poetical works of Gukai Namaççivāyar and his disciples contain Purāṇic episodes set to poetry and music. *Aintokai mālai, Abhirāmi Antāti, Vārāki mālai,* the Soundaryalahirī translations of Vīra Kavirāja Paṇḍitar Kalaigñāna Deepam and several others belong to the later medieval period of Tamil history. 'Tiruppōrūr Sannadi Muṛai' of Çidambaraswāmī of this period is in praise of Lord Muruga, the god of the Tamilians. This is a popular and well recognised work. Saint Tāyumānavar is the towering composer of this period. An enlightened composer, he sought to bring harmony of the souls among Kuru-sects, Śavites, Vétāntins and Śiddar.[11]

Musical compositions of the period between the ninth and fifteenth centuries have not survived. 'Saṅgītaratnākaram' of Śārngadeva (13th century A.D.) mentions about 'Tēvāra Vardani' and a number of paṇs (rāgas) in which Tēvāram is set. Aruṇagirināthar, the giant composer belongs to the fifteenth century. He enriched Tamil music by a new format—by introducing 'Çantam'. He ushered in rythmic patterns. All the lines in this variety of composition strictly confirm to the rhythmic set up of the first, for example, Tana tāna tana tāna tana tāna.[12]

Aruṇāçalakkavirāyar composed the 'Rāmanāṭakam'. Compositions therein are in 'Kīrtanam format' of the eighteenth century. 'Kīrtana' and 'Kṛti' are two terms in common use in the field of Carnātic music. They call for circumscription of boundaries in respect of *lakṣaṇas*. 'Kīrtanam' literally means 'Praises of the Lord'. This format is deemed to be an adaptation of the *Prabandha* form. The transformation of 'prabandha' into 'Kirtana' is said to have taken place during the fourteenth century. In the 'Kīrtana' form the Sāhitya (dhātu) figures conspicuously. Here music is used as a vehicle for conveying a dictum (idea) that is the kernel of the text. The thematic content is invariably religious. *Kīrtanas* are in the form of doxologies wherein the composer expresses his immense devotion to the Lord. Most of the *Kīrtanas* are meant for congregational or group singing.

Kīrtanas are said to be 'Tridhātu Prabhandas' having Pallavī, Anupallavī, and multiple çaraṇas (three aṅgas). In Ékadhātu Kīrtanas, dhātu is made full use of for achieving the *triaṅgas*. In Tridhātu kīrtanas Pallavī and Çaraṇas have different dhātus. *Tridhātu kīrtanas* have different musiċ for Pallavī, Anupallavī and Çaraṇas. If there are multiple Çaraṇas every Çaraṇa has the samė dhātu. Normally, Pallavī and Anupallavī of Kīrtanas have two Āvartas (rhythmic cycles) and four Çaraṇas. The second half of the Çaraṇa is mostly identifiable with the music of Anupallavī. The 'Eḍuppu' (commencement of the three aṅgas) in Kīrtanas is the same. (Samam, Quarter, Half or Three-fourths) Kīrtana is sung as a continuous piece without repetition. Saṅgatīs and Gamakas do not figure profusely in Kīrtanas.[13] Techniques employed for embellishment (Çiṭṭasvaras, Svarasāhitya, Çolkeṭṭu, etc.) are normally absent in Kīrtanas. Some *Kīrtanas* possess literary devices like *Yati*, *Alaṅkāra*, *Prāśa*, and *Svarākṣara*. Each Kīrtana has its own individuality and significance. Utsavaprabhanda kīrtanas, Divyanāma kīrtanas, Utsava-Sampradāya kīrtanas, Navarātri kīrtanas, Pancaratna kīrtānas are examples of them.

Kṛti is another important complex musical form. The composer seeks to combine melody, rhythm and lyric. He makes use of appropriate 'Caṅdas' (metres). A Kṛti is highly music oriented the lyrics taking a secondary place. The composer of a Kṛti has full scope for expressing his thought or feelings.

'Kṛti' is sometimes spoken of as an offshoot of 'Kīrtanam', their roots being traced to Deśī Prabandhams. It is said that Kṛtis became popular during the eighteenth century.[14] The Nāyak and Marātta rule at Tanjāvūr witnessed a large output of Kṛtis. The composer of a Kṛti is free to choose the Rāga. The three aṅgas of a Kṛti (Pallavī/ Anupallavī and Çaraṇa) are supposed to have been modelled after the Prabhandas.[15] Usages of words and syllables match the basic 'Bhāva'. 'Bhakti Rasa' is a conspicuous feature. Wide range of melodies, variety of themes, styles of diction, rhetorical beauty and *rāga-tāḷa* nuances are hallmarks of a well-composed Kṛti. In consideration of the nature of the *Sāhitya, Kṛtis* are classified as *Ékadhātu, Dvidhātu,* and *Tridhātu kṛtis.* Profuse usage of Saṅgatīs and *Gamakas* (Prayōga) is a marked feature. *Sāhitya* serves as a medium to bring out the talent of the composer besides bringing out the musical appeal of the chosen tune (Rāga). Kṛtis have metrical and non-metrical *sāhityas* and they are considered as 'veritable Rāga crystals.' *Saṅgati, Gamaka, Çiṭṭasvara, Madhymakāla Sāhitya, Svarasāhityas, Çolkaṭṭusvara, Svarākṣara* are all embellishing aṅgas (techniques) of a Kṛti. Yamaka, Prāsa, Yati, etc., are all literary beauties.[16] P. Sāmbamūrthy places the origin of the Kīrtana in the latter half of the fourteenth century and according to him a fully developed Kṛti appeared about four centuries later.

The compositions of Aruṇācalakkavirāyar are known as *'Rāmanāṭaka Kīrtanas'.* The incarnation of Lord Viṣṇu as Rāma and the immortal *Rāmāyaṇa* that extols the Lord's glory are favourite themes of poets and scholars. Aruṇāçalakkavi composed the story of Rāma in the form of a musical play in Tamil. Veṅkaṭarāma Iyer and Kōtaṇḍarāma Iyer of Śattanātapuram village helped Kavirāyar in setting appropriate tunes. The compositions abound in prosodical beauties and appeal to the classes and masses.[17]

The dedication of the Bhakti community, the culture of devotion and folk wisdom have been cascading through time and space. The compositions of Tyāgarāja embody the convergence of various currents of Bhakti expression, *Vaiṣṇava, Śaiva*; Sanskrit and colloquial. 'Naukā Çaritram' (1, 7, 10 and 20) echoes the sentiments expressed in scriptures like *Bhāgavata Purāna, Viṣṇu Purāṇa, Gīta Govinda,* Pōtaṇa's Bhāgavatam and also secular poetry such as Çittalapuḍi Yellārya's Rādhā Mādhavam. In traditional oriented society the devotees formed a large loose community, adhered to common practices, and held identical views. Necessarily, a spate of techniques are to be expected. Creation of stereotyped composition is but inevitable. This is not to be mistaken as plagiarism. This uniformity helps blossoming of Bhakti. Some episodes are repeated ad infinitum since they give a cohesion, a homogeneity.

Bhakti ideology is a cultural factor that has an unbroken tradition. This plays a considerable part in influencing compositions of the epoch. This tradition (Bhakti) gets repeated and promulgated. Historical changes do control this trend with turbulence and chaos at times. Fragments (representative of the tradition) that survive, are recreated from the echoes of the past. This accounts for Bhakti-based expressions getting repeated in the compositions. Original sacred impulse and ethos are expressed in many ways particularly in the compositions of Tyāgarāja, the bard of Tiruvaiyāru. The compositions bear witness to the integrity and continuity of the cultural stream.

Tyāgarāja's conception of the exemplary Bhakti centres on the inner experience of relation to the Lord. Other paths like Vedic ritualism, practice of *Haṭayoga* and *Prāṇāyāma, Karma Yoga* too were known. The biographical data and lyrics of Tyāgarāja affirm that he advocates cultivation of spiritual tendencies. The problem of attachment to the divine amidst life's turmoils is the portrayal of a longing devotee, for example, "Ētāvunara-nilakaḍaneeku" in the rāga Kalyāṇī. Many compositions plead with, cajole and demand that the deity should appear before the devotee. Almost fifty per cent of the compositions suggest discontented moods. This is a feeling of desertion (Viraha) and longing. The longing for Darśan of the Lord is expressed in intimate informal terms. (Use of the Telugu expression 'Rā' is in profusion in his songs.) This is a sign of natural intimacy and this is a spontaneous involuntary calling. This reflects the tenor of south Indian Bhakti poetry in vogue whose origins can be traced to earlier epochs. Tyāgarāja expresses the unadulterated charm and ineluctability of the Lord thereby bringing the doctrine of devotion back to life, a doctrine the origins of which could be traced to the time of the *Vaisnavite Ālvārs*, particularly Nammāḻvār. Others are also venerated.

A male often seeks the company of a female, and the Lord concedes (Tanayunibrōva Janani). Tyāgarāja emphasises that the Lord should come in person to bridge the gap that exists between lovers. It is the great Vaisṇavite preceptor Rāmānuja who discussed the concept of "Dayā" (grace). This philosophical postulate was just sprouting when Pillai Lōkāçāriyar and Vedānta Deśikar (author of Dayāsataka A.D. 1269-1370) lived. The Vadakalai branch of Vaiṣṇavite were traditional believers in action for enlisting grace. The Teṅkalaiyar (southerners) were liberals who depended solely on divine grace. Tyāgarāja provides a different imagery. Dependence on dayā does not perclude responsible action on the part of the devotee. (Uraké kalkunā Ramunī Bhakti?) Tyāgarāja contends through a series of questions that people immersed in mundane matters (Samsāra) and who take the fleeting world as real may not become Rāmabhaktas. It must be realised that worldly pleasures are ephemeral. Tyāgarāja observes that 'only those who experience everything as Hari (Lord) can aspire to become Rāmabaktas. This realisation must be a selfless preoccupation. Such compositions emphasize the devotional (value of) chant and the necessity of mental discipline and dedication. Self-stimulation, Viraha sentiment consequent on the separation from the Lord, appeals to the Lord for gifts of the status of a Baṅtu. (Kin) soldier or armed attendant, servant or disciple.

The songs "on worship" (Mānasa Pūjā) interpret all aspects of life in terms of worship and portray a shift from ceremonial religious values to an attempt to infuse in everyday life a feeling of devotion to and dependence on the Lord. This is a genre with precedents by the Haridāsa composers including Vyāsarāja (16th century) and Vijayadāsa as well as Vīrasaivabhakti poets of the Kannaḍa language. Tyāgarāja demonstrates such practices in praxis and encourages others to follow his example.

"Canonical compositions" of saints of the Tamil region (Śaivite Nāyaṅmārs) are the first regular compositions set to music. Nāyaṅmārs in a frenzy expressed their feelings and as such these compositions are spontaneous outpourings. This characteristic method of the exhibition of one's love to a particular form of God registers a greater appeal. *Vaiṣṇava* devotional compositions (Pāśurams of Āḷvārs) are of this variety. But they do not combine the practice of the attendant arts as the Saiva devotional works do. The dates of these canonical saints are still enveloped in a maze. In the compositions of Tyāgarāja, there are cognizable evidences of the influence of the Nāyaṅmārs and Āḷvārs. Carnātic music in the Tamil region seems to have been watered by the native norms that have been popular before the advent of the Trinity.

Muttuswāmī Dīkṣitar, Tyāgarāja and Śyāma-Śāstrī through their compositions make significant contributions to the fields of music, religion and spiritual pursuit. Compositions of Dīkṣitar are scholarly. When we think of the numberless pilgrimages that he undertook the purposiveness with which he sang on the numerous shrines of Śiva and Viṣṇu, we may call him a sixty-fourth Nāyanār or the thirteenth Āḷvār. He is a favourite child of Lord Guruguha (Muruka) and in this respect he can be deemed as a second Aruṇagiri. When he speaks of Yantras, he appears to be Bhāskararāya reincarnating for spreading the *Tāntric* cult. Speaking of the Mother, Dīkṣitar states that Her two breasts are 'sweet poetry and music'. (Sarasa-saṅgīta sāhitya stāna dvaya—the kīrtana in the rāga çāya gauḷa). The fit object of adoration by the art of music is God Himself and no mortal.

Dīkṣitar refers to himself as a Vaiṇika gāyaka, a vocalist and master of Vīṇā. (Bālagopāla in the rāga Bhairavī). He also describes himself as a Paṇḍita-tara. (Pārvatī Paraméśvaram vandé in the rāga Bhauḷi). These references provide the requisite clue for understanding the art of Dīksitar. He illustrates the science of *Rāga*, *Mela*, *Janya,* etc., and he speaks of *Mantras, Tantras*, and philosophies.

The Advaidic sanyāsin of Kānchīpuram, Upaniṣad Brahman himself a composer, seems to have exercised profound influence on Dīkṣitar. Evidently, Muttuswāmi Dīkṣitar is steeped in the musical heritage of Tamil Nadu.

Ghanam Kṛṣṇa Iyer and Ghaṇam Subbarāma Iyer have contributed 'Padams'. Kīrtanas and Padams of Muttutāṇḍavar and Mārimuttu Piḷḷai are popular in the music and dance performances of Tamil Nadu. A musical monologue 'the Padam' is a simple structure which has high literary and musical value. 'Padam' has a meaningful sāhitya. This variety is also one of the aṅgas of prabhanda describing the heroic qualities of the Nāyaka (hero). 'Pada' is sometimes considered as an offshoot of 'Tāḷa prabandha', a variety in the regional language. Nāyaka-Nāyikā Bhāva is the basic theme for Padas, Pada-varṇas, Kṛtis, Jāvaḷis and Gēya-nāṭakas. Padas extoll the greatness and sanctity of 'Madhura Bhakti'. The heroes and heroines in Padas are given the status of Paramātmā Lord and Jīvātmā (devotee). Śakhi is the preceptor (guru). The theme of Madhura Bhakti gains perfection in Padams.

Padam compositions combine 'Bāhya Śrngāra' (explicit love) and Aṅtara Bhakti (inner devotion). Padams have as their Nāyaka Lord Kṛṣṇa, Naṭarāja and Subrahmaṇya (Murukan).

Aikya and Vedānta rahasya are at the root of Padam philosophy. The texts often convey 'Soundarya-garvitā' (beauty-conscious Nāyaka), anger, jealousy, sarcasm, expectancy, depression, mundane love, aggressiveness, self-aberration, boasting, etc. Varieties of Śṛṅgāra rasa such as Saṁboga, Vipralaṁba, Ayoga, Saṁpanna-saṁyoga are found in the Pada compositions. Some Pada compositions also provide information about plants, medicines, jewels, trees and herbs.

As a musical form Pada has commendable merit. Pleasing and popular rāgas are selected for providing tune. The rāgas suggest the underlying *Bhāva* and Rasa. Facile beats (Miśra-çāpu, Ādi and Rūpakam) are used often. The tempo (Layam) is mostly slow (Viḷambika and Madhya degree). Padams can be taken as examples of 'Tridhātu Prabandhas'.[18] Padams of Ghanam Kṛṣṇa Iyer and Subbarama Iyer are extensively used in dance. The tempo of the Padams enable the dancer to improvise 'light foot' steps. Scope for gamaka prayōgas and Saṅgatis are limited in Padams.

Ānai Ayya is another well-known composer of the period. Gopālakṛṣṇa Bhāratī has earned immortal fame by composing the 'Naṅdanār Çaritram' based on the story of Tiruppāṇāḷvar in the Periyapurāṇam of Śekkiḷār. Gopālakrsna Bhāratī learnt music under Rāmdoss of Hindustānī tradition and Ghanam Kṛṣṇa Iyer of Carnātic tradition.[19] He imbibed the spirit of the Maharashtra 'Hari katha' and later adapted it to the genius of the Tamil language. By simple living and yogic practices he felt one with the highest and the lowest and was in due course greatly respected by the masses and classes. He composed many in the folk-style such as Kummi, Kōḷāttam, Lāli, Ūñjal and Nalaṅku. He composed songs for the children. The musical mould resembles Tyāgarāja's, as it had more music and less words. Bhāratī bequeathed to Indian culture a rich heritage of spirituality and artistry.

'Kuṛavaṅçi' is a new form that emerges at this point of time. This variety incorporates music, dance and drama. Kuṛṛālakkuṛavaṅçi of Tirukūṭa rāśappa-Kavirāyar and Alaṅkārakkuṛavañci of Kavi Kuñjara Bhāratī are well known. In 'Kuravañci', the classical and folk tunes are pressed into service. Maḷavai Çidambara Bhāratī and Rāmaswāmī Śivan (Guhadāsan) composed in Tamil.

Aṇṇāmalai Reddiyar of Chennimalai is the well known author of the variety of composition known as 'Kāvaḍi-Çiṅtu'. Subramanya Bhāratī, widely known for his patriotic songs is a composer of great merit. He had made use of the Kāvaḍi-ciṅtu format of Aṇṇāmalai Reddiyar, folk-forms like Kiḷikkanni, Ānantaḳkaḷippu, etc. Nīlakaṇṭa Śivan, Lakṣmaṇa Piḷḷai, Muthia Bāgavatar, Acyuta Dāśar, and Māyūram Viswanātha Sāstri are well known composers of relatively recent years. Viswanatha Sāstri has set Tirukkuṛal to music.[20] Koteeśvara Iyer (b. 1862) lived to a ripe old age of seventy-six. In 1920, he took upon himself the onerous task of composing in all the seventy-two mēlakartas.

Three views about Meḷakartas were current at the time of Koteeśvara Iyer. One school felt that only thirty-two of them could be sung and the other forty to be discarded as they were subject to Vivādī-dōsa.[21] Another school was of the view that the Vivādī meḷas need not be discarded but they should be sung in 'Vakra' and 'Varjya' prayōgas to escape 'Vivādī-dōṣa'. Veṅkaṭamakin, the father of the seventy-two meḷakarta scheme seems to have anticipated the tangle. A third school held that all the seventy-two melakartas had musical potentialities and they could and should be sung as straight sampūrṇa rāgas. Koteeśvara Iyer had conceived the idea of treating all the méḷakartas as straight Sampūrna rāgas. At the time of Koteeśvara Iyer's venture, most of the compositions of Tyāgarāja (kṛtis) in the Vivādī meḷa do not seem to have gained circulation. He could not have derived any positive guidance from Muttuswāmī Dīkṣitar who treated them in 'Vakra' and 'Varjya' prayōgas. The Meḷa-rāga mālika of Mahā Vaidyanātha Iyer could not have helped him much.[22] The rāgas therein are not dealt with in full campus. Koteeśvara Iyer's compositions bristle with svarākṣara saṅdhi and he has introduced rāga name, in each of the mēlakarta kṛtis.[23]

The output of Pāpanāśam Śivan of recent memory is impressive. He brought 'classical music' to the common man by his inimitable compositions to the films. Many composers in Tamil like Pāpanāśam Śivan have made valuable contributions to language and music. In regions other than Tamil Nadu also such contributions have also been made. The 'Sōpāna type' of Kerala is a slow and majestic flow, pregnant with devotion. In different styles of different States, i.e. Āndhra, Karnātaka, Mahārāştra, Gujārat, Punjāb, Bengal, and Orissa we can notice individual characteristics and excellences. Devotional compositions outnumber other types.

Musical compositions are poems and have wider appeal. Rhyming of syllables in the required metre is a commendable exercise. Literary beauties adorning compositions are Yati, Prāsa, Yamaka, etc. They lend charm and value to the compositions. Sāhityas bristle with literary embellishments. 'Yamaka' is a variety of rhyme. The same text gives different shades of meaning and sense. 'Yamaka' is known in Tamil literary convention as 'Matakku'. 'Prāsas' are life-giving syllables for poetry. A single syllable is repeated either at the beginning or middle (second syllable) or at the end (Anuprāśa, Dvideeyākṣara prāsa or Antya prāsa). Adoption of prāsa in a composition reveals the literary genius and scholarship of the composer. 'Yati' is a variety of Dhātu-Mātu Alaṅkāra' and concerns the sphere of Svara and Sāhitya. This is repetition of the same word, phrase or syllable many times in an ordained manner. It may also be defined as 'the letter that occurs after a pause at the middle of the Tāḷa-āvarta-padaçcēta'. This is known as 'Mōnai' in Tamil literary convention. Taking into consideration the nature of Yati phrases, they are classified as Gōpuçça Yati, Srōta-vāha, Mrdaṅga Yati, Sama Yati and Viṣama Yati. Introduction of Yati in musical compositions calls for competence in literature and music.

This survey of compositions in music (particularly of the composers of Tamil Nadu) brings into fore certain interesting hypotheses. Compositions of the pre-Trinity period place more emphasis on the language (text). Medieval compositions (Prabandhas, Śūlādis, etc.) have more musical appeal. Paitāla Gurumūrti Sāstri is a composer of Geetas who belongs to the pre-Trinity period. Sonṭi Veṅkaṭasubbiah, Paccimiryam Ādiyappiah, Pallavī Gōpala Iyer, Kavi-Mātrubūtayya, Çaukkam Veerabhadrayya, Mārgadarśī Śēṣa Iyengār, have to their credit compositions which can be classified as a variety midway (between Kīrtanas and Kṛtis.) *Dhātu-Mātu alankara* is counted as one of the characteristics of Kṛti to be ranked as classical. Rāmaswāmī Dīkṣitar's 'Chandasēla' in the rāga Hamsadvani is an example of medieval Prabhanda.

Saṅgīta Sārāmṛta of King Tuḷaja (A.D. 1735) gives an idea of the quality of music current in his times. This work stimulated great enthusiasm at a time when the Trinity made their entry in to the arena. The 'Krti' form is consolidated leaving nothing for further improvement. Tyāgarāja had made use of both the Kṛti and Kīrtana formats. His Kīrtanas are Sāhitya oriented and his Kṛtīs have a blend of Sāhitya and Saṅgīta. Tyāgarāja's Pañca-ratna Kṛtīs give the idea that he could have been an adept composer of *Tāna-varnas.*

Śyāma Śāstrī gives us examples of Svarajati and Tāna-varna. He remains content with the choice of some popular rakti-rāgas. A.D. 1850 is an era of evolution of rāga-forms. Tyāgarāja and Muttuswāmi Dīkṣitar have fully utilised the knowledge of rāgas; and their compositions are 'rāga crystals'. Scales are legion but rāgas have to be created out of them. Tyāgarāja and Dīkṣitar drew succour from the past and transmitted them to posterity. They made use of compositions as channels.

Music served as the best medium for the composers to give expression to their feelings. Besides enriching the art of music, composers also increased literary output. Rhymes, alliterations rhetorics, figures of speech, etc., were made use of for enriching the language. Setting compositions in particular metres, and specifying appropriate tāḷas show the degree of skill they had acquired in the art of composing. The 'Dviteeyākṣara prāsa' (second letter rhyming) is the gift of the *Nāyanmārs* and *Āḷvārs* of Tamil tradition. From the time of composers like Mārgadarśī Seṣa Iyeṅgar, this technique gains much popularity. It should be noted that Jeyadeva the composer of Aṣṭapatis had not adopted this technique. Jeyadēva blends music and poetry making use of 'middle and end rhyme' and Yamakas which were popular with Sanskrit poets.

Talappākkam Annamāçārya's Kīrtanas in the Telugu language contain a Pallavī and Çaraṇas. (A.D. 1424 to 1503). The compositions of Śrī-Pada Rāya and Vyāsa Rāya in the Kannada language are called 'Padas'. These bear a close resemblance to Annamāçārya's Kīrtanas. Annamāçārya makes use of Dviteeyāksara prāsa. It is also to be remembered that Annamāçārya is the author of 'Saṅkīrtana Lakṣaṇamu'.[24]

Haridāsas introduced new varieties of compositions like Śūlāti, *Ugāboga, Devarnāma, Vrittanāma, Udayarāga*, etc. They use similies, metaphors and Śabdālankāras. *Post-Puraṅdara dāsa* period witnesses rise of illustrious composers like Nārāyaṇa Tīrta, Sadāśiva Brahmēṅdra, and Ūttukkāḍu Veṅkaṭasubbier. Nārāyaṇa Tīrta's Kṛṣṇalīlātarangiṇī is the longest musical drama in Sanskrit containing one-hundred and forty-seven Taraṅgams (kīrtanas); two hundred and sixty-seven ślōkas; thirty gadyams and thirty Darūs besides prose passages.[25]

It is possible to arrange the compositions of Sadāśiva Brahmendra chronologically by a critical study of his life-history. A hypothetical analysis of the saint's life suggests that his compositions on Lord Kṛṣṇa must have emerged at the moment of his entry into ascetic life. These are followed by compositions on Śrī Rāmā, marked by 'Śānti' and 'Bhakti'. Rāma's divinity is well brought out. Brahmendra's capacity to visualise Rāmā's prowess is admirable. Ultimate transition to asceticism becomes apparent in compositions like 'Kēḷati mama hṛdayé'(Lord sports in my heart of hearts). The Ātman merges with the Supreme Power and the Kṛtis that come chronologically later appear to be 'Ānanda Poorna bōdēyam'. In these Kṛtis he claims to have attained complete enlightenment. Immortal compositions of Brahmendra fascinate and charm lovers of spiritual literature in Sanskrit. The compositions are tilting and rhythmic, but we do not know whether the rāgas (tunes) in which they are sung today are the saint's creation.

The compositions of Mārgadarśī Śeṣa Iyeṅger earn him the reputation of 'Pathfinder' (Mārgadarśī). Highlighting the Śabdālaṅkāra nuances of Śēṣa Iyeṅger the Māhārāja of Travancore Svāti Tirunāl wrote a monograph in Sanskrit namely 'Muhanna prāsa Antyaprāsa-Vyavasta'.[26] Svāti Tirunāḷ's Kṛti 'Bhōgeendra Sāyinam' is a close imitation of Śēṣa Iyeṅgar's composition 'Śrīreṅga Śāyinam' if assessed on the basis of phrasing and construction.

Saṅgīta Sampradāya Pradarśinī of Subbarāma Dīkṣitar contains critical observations on the qualities of a 'Vākgeyakāra'.[27] Any person who composes 'Mātu' (text) and sets the Dhātu (tune) is a composer of music.[28] An ideal composer is one who possesses a detailed knowledge of the science of grammar. The composer must be a past-master well-acquainted with knowledge contained in the lexicons, the science of prosody dealing with metres, poetics, figures of speech, the nine rasas, sixty-four arts, knowledge of rhythmic patterns and instinct (Pradibha) to innovate. These qualities are essential for a 'Dhātu-Mātu kāra' (Ideal Vākgeyakāra).

If a composer packs his compositions with words that malign the Dhātu, despite his possessing knowledge of Dhātu and Mātu lacks the potential to compose Prabandhas. He is to be classified as 'Madyama Vākgēyakāra' (Average). Having composed an excellent Mātu, if he is unable to provide an equally good Dhātu, that composer is an 'Adhama Vākgēyakāra' (mediocre). If one composes Dhātu and Mātu just to match the theme, he is known as 'Vāstu Kavi' (exemplary composer). If a composer satisfies himself with description of events and situations he is termed a 'Varṇa Kavi' (adept describer). He comes under the category of Madhyma-Vākgēyakāra. One who frames up a suitable tune confirming to varnakrama to a text authored by another person; as well as one who frames up a fitting tune to the Pallavī (initial part) without altering the rest of the text they are also classified as average composers.

Throughout the world the earliest music is 'Sacred music'. Evidently it is definitely earlier than secular music. The music compositions in south India are both sacred and secular. Much of the techniques of the early Tamil composers seem to have been absorbed into the general stream of 'Carnātic music'. Between fifth and seventh centuries A.D., Śaivite and Vaiṣṇavite composers poured forth verses in Tamil. They were set to music and rendered with or without rhythm. Such compositions form an integral part of the current Carnātic music repertoire. Nāṭyaśāstra of Bharata mentions about Druvas and Gītis. Mataṅga mentions about forty-nine Deśī prabandhas. Śārṅgadēva mentions about seventy-five different Prabandhas.[29] Prabandhs were replaced by varieties of compositions which constitute the core of Carnātic music compositions handled today.

Kirtana in an embryonic form appeared in the fourteenth century A.D. The Dāsas (Śrī Pāda Rāya, Vyāsarāya and others) the fore-runners of Purandaradāsa (A.D. 1484 to 1564). Purandaradāsa's contribution is enormous and ranges from graded exercises to beginners to superquality sublime compositions.[30]

The Talappākkam composers of Andhra deśa contributed Kīrtanas in the Telugu language. Generous royal patrons particularly of the Tanjore court consolidated the heritage. Krtis gain the upperhand since then. A galaxy of minor composers of the post-Trinity period keep the torch aglow and enrich the repertoire.

Though different languages are used, the role of Sanskrit can never be underestimated. The Padas of the Dāsakūta composers contain profuse use of Sanskrit words.[31] Annamāçārya a close contemporary of the Dasakūṭas, uses Sanskrit as a medium as evidenced by some of his compositions.[32] Among the pre-Trinity composers Mārgadarśī Śēṣa Iyengar is a great Sanskrit scholar. Many of his compositions are in Sanskrit and they bear the stamp (Mudra/Aṅkita) 'Kōsala'. Maharaja Svāti Tirunāl in his work 'Muhanna prāsa aṅtya prāsa' discusses how alliterations at the beginning, middle and end of the lines of a composition should be handled. As illustrations the royal author quotes from the compositions of Mārgadarśī Śēṣa Iyeṅgar. The well-known Tiruppukaḷ compositions of saint Aruṇagirināthar in the Tamil language show deft handling of Sanskrit phrases and words. Muttuswāmī Dīkṣitar composed in Sanskrit and Śyāma Śāstrī and Tyāgarāja use Sanskrit words.[33] Muttuswāmī Dīkṣitar's compositions are moulded in classical style displaying deep scholarship. Beautiful words and sound phrases. Of the composers of recent memory particular mention must be made of Kōṭeeśvara Iyer and Māyūram Viśwanātha Śāstri.[34]

Classical compositions are those which conform to certain exactitude of form, the imprint of each easily denotes sanctity of the rāga, a perfect sense of laya and excellence of Sāhitya. *Bhāva, Rāga, Tāḷa* the three composite elements which go to make a *Krti* meet the challenges of aesthetic appeal, and specify a particular song (composition) as belonging to a classical mould. The expression 'classical' in one sense means 'having permanent interest and value' and in another 'music written in a particular style aiming at the embodiment of certain ideal, the chief element of which is beauty of form'. Kṛti is therefore the work of a composer who had cared for all the norms of classical quality. Compositions are the *pellucid* springs of spontaneous aesthetic experience and the inner sanctuary of true devotion. Often the richest harvest of spiritual satisfaction is derived from the classical purity and fecund originality of great composers.

REFERENCES

1. L'arc, 40, p.17.
2. Cage: Silence and satisfaction, p.10.
3. Claude Levi Strauss: The Raw and the Cooked Note 119, p.18.
4. Sigmund Freud: The Moses of Michael Angelo. (Standard Education (Tr) James Strachey Vol.13, London, Hogarth, 1958) p. 2{1.
5. T.V. Kuppuswami: Carnatic music and the Tamils. (Kaliṅga Publications, Delhi, 1992).
6. Popularly known as 'Śaṅgam Literature'.
7. V.Pa.Ka. Sundaram: Tolkāppiyattil Iśaikkurippu. (International Institute of Tamil Studies, 1994).
8. Tiruvaḷḷuvar had followed the Tolkāppiyam dictum "Annilai maruṅkin aram mutaliya (ākia) muṃmutar porutkumariya enpa. (Tolkāppiyam 1363).
9. Tirugñāna Sambandar, the boy saint of Sīrkāḷi is one of the Tēvāram trio.
   T.V. Kuppuswami: *op. cit.,* Chapter IV.
10. Vaḷḷi Ammāḷ, a native of Tirukkāttāmpuliyūr (Carnātic music and the Tamils: *op. cit.*) p. 83.
11. Compositions of Siddar like Kutampai Siddar and Pāmpātti Siddar contain philosophical truths couched in simple melodies.
    Eg: 'Mānkōi Pāluṇḍu' of Kutampai Siddar.
12. T.V. Kuppuswami and T.K. Venkatasubramanian: Rhythm in Historical Cognition. (Kalinga Publications, Delhi 91) Appendix.
13. The purpose of introducing 'Saṅgatīs' is to make explicit certain delicate musical aspect and latent shades of meaning in the Sāhitya. Saṅgatīs are improvised by Vākgēyakāras themselves or by eminent musicians who handle the compositions. *Saṅgatis* should be in perfect unison with the general tenor of the text (Sāhitya). Tyāgarāja, Muttuswāmī Dīkṣītar, Māṛgadarśi Śeṣa Iyengar, Annamāchārya, Badrācalam Rāmadāsar, Sadāśiva Brahmēndra, Pāpanaśam Śivan, Ūttukkāḍu Veṅkaṭasubbier, Gopalakṛṣṇa Bhāratī, Nīlakaṇṭha Śivan, Svāti Tirunāl Mahārāja, Iraiyimman Thampi are considered as kīrtanakāras. *Gamaka*: It is a musical embellishment possessing delicate nuances and shades. It is a decorative aspect that adorns the Dhātu of Kṛtis. The 'shaking' of the svara is attempted in such a way that the musical excellence of the composition is enhanced. Gamaka adorns a musical composition just as jewellery adorn a lady. It lends life to the rāga. Gamakas add to the melodic beauty of Carnātic musical forms. Also : Supra : Ch. I.
14. This is debatable. Confused chronology is the result of vague definitions of 'Kṛti and kīrtana'. Which is earlier in point of time is a moot question,

since there is a great deal of overlapping in defining the concepts.

15. They are claimed to be inherited from *Udgrahamēlāpaka* and *Abhōga* of Geeta Prabandhas.

16. P. Sambamurthy : A Dictionary of South-Indian Music and Musicians. Volume II (The Indian Publishing House, Madras 14, 1984), pp. 338-39.

17. Tunes set by Veṅkaṭarāma Iyer and Kotaṇdarāma Iyer are not available to us. The date of Kavirāyar is taken as A.D. 1712 to 1779 A.D. Popular tunes (Kēdāra Gouḷa for Antarāma Soundaryam; Surati for Kāṇavēṇum lakṣam kaṇkaḷ; Bairavi for 'Yārō ivar Yāro, etc.) seem to be contributions of later day musicians. Late Ariyakkudi Ramanuja Iyengar set tune to many of the compositions.

18. The Dhātu for Pallavī, Anupallavī and first half of Carana usually has the music of the Anupallavi. There are also Group Padas like Group Kṛtis dedicated to particular deities.

19. Tiruviḍaimarutūr was then the enlightened seat of such activities patronised by the Marātta prince Amarasimha. Rāmdōss and Kṛṣṇa Iyer were court-vidwāns. (Āstāna Vidwāns).

20. Professor V.V. Ṣaṭakopan formerly of the Delhi University set tune Tirukkuḷal couplets by restructuring them in Kṛti format.

21. *Vādi* : The dominant note in a Rāga or a svara phrase. This is considered as the kingpin of melody.

    Vivādi :The dissonant note which has a discordant effect. It is deemed as enemical to melody.

    Samvādi : A consonant note which bears a concordant relationship with Vādi or Tonic note in comparison with the music.

    Mēḷakarta : Associated with Veṅkatamakin and covers a sequence of rāgas of the 'past, present and future'.

22. Mahā Vaidyanatha Iyer composed it in praise of Lord Praṇatārtihara. Çiṭṭasvaras are appended after each Kaṇṭa (çakra). Each stanza has six melas in it.

23. *Svarākṣara*:This is Dhātu-Mātu alaṅkāra where svara and sāhitya are of the same syllable. This is applicable only to vocal music.

24. Work edited by Dr. Selva Krishnamurthy under the title 'Tunes of Divinity' (Institute of Asian Studies, Madras).

25. B. Natarajan: Kṛṣṇalīlātarangini of Nārāyana Tīrta. (Tr) (Mudgala Trust. 'Kaveri' 12. IV Cross Street, R.K. Nagar, Madras 28).

26. Published by the Music Academy, Madras.

27. Saṅgita Sampradāya Pradarśini, (Telugu, Volume I, 1904. (Tr) T.S. Pārthasārathi. Rendered into English by P.K. Rājagōpāla Iyer).

28. "Vāṅmātruçyaete gēyam dhāturityabhideeyate/Vāçam geyam ça kurute yassavākgeyakāraka : *(Ibid.)*

29. 'Prabandha' literally means anything that is 'well-knit'.

30. These include Gīta, *Thāyam, Prabandha, Śūlādi, Ūgābhōga, Padya*, and *Dēvarnāma*.
31. 'Nandanandana Pāhi' of Śrī-Pāda Rāya in the *rāga Brindāvana Sāranga*.
32. "Namo Nārāyaṇāya nama :" (Saṅgīrtana in the rāga Tilang).
33. Spiritual heritage of Tyāgarāja, (R.K. Mutt, Mylapore, 1957) Introduction.
34. Krti of Koteeśvara Iyer 'Kārunya Kaṇda Gñānāmrtam' in the rāga Dhavalāmbari (49th Méla).

    Krti of Mayūram Viśvānatha Śāstri 'Jeyati Jeyati Bhāratamāta in the rāga Khamās'.

4

Historical Contextuality

"The instinct to record sound is one of the three essential powers of the Gods in ancient societies along with that of making war and causing famine."[1] Music (sound) however presents very special problems.[2] The disciplined progress registered by Carṇātic music is due to adherence to injunctions envisaged by classical treatises. Sōmanātha author of 'Rāgavibhōda' for instance prefaces his work with the couplet:

"Rāgavibhōdam nidate virōda rōdāya
Lakşya Lakṣaṇayō"

Sōmanātha claims that he is evolving a crisp text of Lakṣaṇa and Lakṣya music eschewing all prevailing controversies. Mataṅga refers to Kāśyapa, Kōhala, Dattila Durgāśakti, Naṅdikēśvara, Nārada, Bharata, Yastika, Viśvasau, Sārdūla and Veṇu.[3] References are not to names only. Mataṅga supplies information about views expressed by earlier theorists. For instaṅce, Mataṅga quotes Bharata's Nāṭyaśāstra and the passages he quotes are not available in other similar texts (recensions) of Nāṭyaśāstra.[4] The information provided by Mataṅga's text can be summarised: (a) Bharata had omitted Ma-Ni pairs from Samvādi. Mataṅga mentions seven Śrutis (intervals) representing Sāmvāda, (b) Sa-Ma are mentioned as Grāmāṇi svaras of the Ṣadjagrāma and Madhyagrāma respectively, (c) furnishes etymological definitions of svara sṛuti, Mūrçana, Jāti, etc., (d) discusses mutual relationship between svara and Śṛuti, (e) uses symbolic syllables for the seven svaras (Sa, Ri, Ga, Ma and so on). Phonetic notation of Vedic hymn is replaced by a new method making provision for elongated notes (Sā, Rī, Gā, Mā, etc.), (f) illustrates Grāma and Mūrçana by charts, (g) elucidates

Bharata's treatment of the subject of demonstrative process of Śrutis, (h) discusses the concepts of Mārgī and Deśī and classification (treatment of Deśī rāgas however have not been recorded), (i) classifies forty-nine Prabandhas into Sūda, Ālikrama and Prakīrṇa, (j) deals with Gīta and Vādya independently of Nāṭya.

Śrikaṇṭha, the author of 'Rasakaumudī' is another theorist of medieval times who motivates theoretical studies.[5] He mentions the names of some of the chronologically earlier authors but strangely is silent about his immediate predecessors.[6] 'Rasakaumudī' is an important medieval treatise which bears ample evidence of the replacement of some of the characteristics of the ancient system by incoming innovations. Few of the observations could be summarised: (a) 'Śṛīkaṇṭha accepts seven Vikṛti svaras but omits Kākaḷi niṣāda and Antara gāndhāra admitted by Rāmamātya[7]. This perhaps is due to the reconciliation of svara names of Śārṅgadéva which were applicable to *Grāma-mūrcana* system with the system of twelve fixed notes in an octave. (b) Ṣadja is taken as tonic.[8] (c) 'Śrīkaṇṭha closely follows *Rāmamātya* when he introduces Vīṇa (instrument) as the medium of manifestation of rāgas. He describes the tuning of strings and location of svaras on the frets. He elaborates on the technique of Viṇa play (Vādana Bhéda). This is derived from information provided by Saṅgītaratnākaram.[9] (d) Treatment of Rāga classification is a combination of 'Mela classification' (south) and 'Rāga-rāginī classification' (north).[10] Yet Śrīkaṇṭha is not the pioneer to gain distinction of conceiving a synthesis of Meḷa and Rāga-rāgini systems. Rāgādhyāya of Śrīkaṇṭha's work lists svaras of each mela and rāga and gives brief details of Graha, Aṁśā, Nyāsa, Alpatva, Bahutha, Varjya svaras, sometimes, Rasa and Mūrcana of rāgas.[11] (e) Śrīkāṇṭha also refers to the classification of rāgas as Auḍava, Ṣāḍava, Çāyālaga and Sampūrṇa as well as Sudda, Çāyalagā and Sankīrṇa. (f) He mentions six principal rāgas as appropriate to six seasons and the association of different periods of the cycle of day and night with six seasons. (g) Gamaka, Śārīrā, Gāyani, defects of Vākgeyakāras, six kinds of çāyas, stāyisvara, ālāpti, vulnerability of musicians are all dealt with.[12]

The random samples (ancient and medieval) bear witness to the continued wisdom evinced by the authors in the theory of music. The derivation (Vyutpatti) and usage (Pravṛautti) of original Sanskrit terms have much to convey.[13] Interpreting sāstras in terms of laksyas is exacting. 'Saṅgīta Śāstra' and 'Śāstrīya Saṅgīta' cannot be equated with English terms 'musicology' and 'classical music'. 'Śāstrīya Saṅgīta' is a misnomer because it follows lakṣaṇas not necessarily embodied in Śāstras alone, but also in 'Oral Sampradāya' (tradition?) Lakṣaṇas embodied in treatises (Śāstras) motivate, perhaps generate oral tradition.

Information that treatises provide are to be classified as historical, arithmetical, scientific, geographical and pedagogical. A conscious contemplation would prove that 'levels of aesthetic experience' motivated development of idea of Rāgas, Bhāva, and Rasa representing three levels in the ascending order of excellence in the experience in relation to music. To reduce them to capsules of theoretic proportions is a delicate endeavour. Our ancients have achieved remarkable success in meeting the challenge and we are the beneficiaries of the results recorded. Lack of appreciation and uninhibited recognition of the levels of musical talent, will deprive musical satisfaction and musical fulfilment.

Frontiers of music study are expanding. The Śāstrakāras (Musicologists?) have provided the material to ruminate. To effectively digest the material there is need to evolve a scheme. The contents of the proposed study scheme could be classified as (a) Codification of musical practices, (b) Study of social relation to music, (c) Study of music materials. According to ancients 'sound' is a quality of breath (air-Śvāsa). Audible sound was 'Dhvani'. Transcendental sound was 'Sphoṭa'. Bharata spoke of Sṛtis in relation to music of his times. All ancestors (Śāstrakāras) have made valuable contributions to the 'Science of Sound'. In dealing with material out of which 'Music' is produced (sound), production, propagation and perception (of sound) are studied. Incentives to music, mechanism of perceiving music out of a set of tones also form parts of the study.[14] But the 'measurement of all pitches of perception and Gamakas in the singing of a rāga say Mōhanam is really beyond the scope.[15] Pitch variations like the vibrate and trills are below the conscious. "They can be experienced only in some cases and that too with great concentrated effort."[16] P. Sambamurthy is of the view that musicology includes the study of every topic pertaining to music minus actual performance. His emphasis in on 'musical pedagogy'.

Ethnomusicology is a branch of the scientific study of music. Music has grown as the natural expression of the particular genius of a particular people or nation. Ethnomusicology is the study of the music envisaged as part of the culture of a particular human group, race or nation. It is not correct to say that it means the study of tribal or primitive music and the established system of art-music is too lofty to be probed into with the help of modern norms. Atleast four entirely distinct systems of music (Matās) have existed in India. There is confusion as to the essential elements of each Matā. Studying music as a human phenomenon is not altogether new. The very title of Matanga's work is 'Bṛhaddeśī. It reveals the intention of the author of studying varieties of men's music just as they are preserved by the people of the land. Ethnomusicology plays a role in music studies as archaeology in history. It provides the documents (positive) enabling us to verify and implement the data received from written and oral tradition. It may reveal the possible direction in which a particular system of music can develop taking the line of its original genius.

In a particular sense history of music is the history of what we use as practical exponents of the art. It could be analysed in terms of pedagogically-laid exercises and grammar as well as an aesthetically evolved art according to certain norms quite outside the jurisdiction of pedagogy. Musicology will serve as a telescope and a microscope. For the progress (motivation) of music and its sustenance from within 'scientific study' is certainly a fertilizer and pesticide. Music criticism does not come under the purview of scientific study of music. Longfellow's observations pertaining to literature deserve notice : "Some critics are like chimney sweepers; they put on the fire below and frighten the swallows from their nests above; they scrape for a long time in the chimney, cover themselves with soot and bring nothing away but a bag of cinders and then sing out from the top of the house as if they had built it."

A bio-cultural fusion between east and west did take place with the adoption of the musical instrument violin. This fusion provided motivation of an unprecedented scale. Music is only one aspect of the coming together of civilisations and the lovers of Indian music wonder which way the inevitable developments would be. In the West too music has gone through periods of staggering changes and upheavels. From the eleventh century polyphonic experiments lured more composers to try out bold combinations of apparently totally unrelated melody. Contrary to fears expressed by contemporaries, Europe witnessed flowering of polyphonic perfection in the centuries that followed. Subsequently, this prolific development changed in the course of few centuries to the mighty musical structure of the nineteenth century through Beethoven, Wagner and a host of others. In our own days new formats of serial music and other varieties invited challenges. Perhaps some of the connoisseurs felt, as we do now, that this was death-knell to music itself. But music is very much alive there. In Europe the next generation was moved by Schoenberg, who even twenty-five years ago was considered as a 'Maker of nothing but barren theoretical fabrications which might possibly speak to the brain not to the heart'.

Indian norms expect music to be emotional and aesthetic. In our rāga-ālāpanas we have no use for words. In such types of compositions in which though the words and their sense have value, the primary emphasis is on rāga-swarūpa, and rhythmic beauty. In compositions where the primary appeal is to emotion, the pangs of a lover, the exploits of a hero, or sufferings of a person is portrayed. The 'Sāhitya' (text) evokes Śṛṅgāra rasa in one case, Vīra rasa in another and Karuṇā in one more context. In such instances music properly harnessed, maximises emotion. Tune employed is simple and direct, not ornate or elaborate. In other words emphasis is on the text and their sense, music serving as a handmaid.

Religious music dominate the repertoire of Carnātic system. Sages and poets since Vedic times have stressed the role of Bhakti in salvaging the human soul. The earliest music extant is what is found in the Tēvāram hymns of Śaivite nāyanmārs and Divyaprabandham of Vaiṣṇavite āḷvārs.[17] These compositions are simple in structure. Structural refinement is met with in the *Dē-varnāmas* of *Dāsakūṭas* in the Kannada language. These compositions of the *Dāsakūṭas* have a *Pallavī*, and number of Caraṇas, melody of every caraṇa being the same. This variety dates back to the tenth century A.D. This format had become pan-Indian as evidenced by 'Gīta-gōvindam' of Jeyadeva. (Astapati). Aṣtapatis are modelled after the Dévarnāmas. Purandaradāsa, claimed as the "Father of Carnātic Music" was influenced by this variety of 'Religious music'. The total number of rāgas made use of in rendering Dévarnāmas is around fifty. Mostly they are rakti rāgas inspiring the sentiment of Bhakti. Purandaradāsa's Dēvarnāmas has influenced the bard of Tiruvaiyāru namely Tyāgarāja and Muttuswāmī Dīkṣitar. By adopting Māyāmāḷawa Gowḷa rāga for initiation into Carnātic music Purandaradāsa had brought in a radical change in outlook. Since the days of Purandaradāsa innumerable formats (compositions) have been brought into the music arena.[19]

In the manner of construction and shape, musical instruments differ. Acquiring skill in the play of these instruments needs practice in the play of the compositions. Manipulating techniques have been dealt with elaborately in treatises. In all these, vocal rendering of the compositions serves as a guiding factor (Gāyaki style). Limitations in the play of the instrument warrant special Tchniques and consequently the shape of the melody gets changed sometimes. In the field of Carnātic music the place of the Vīnā as an accompanying instrument had been usurped by the violin. Claims of the Indian origin of the violin are not universally accepted.[20] The discussion of origin mostly centres round the origin of the bow.[21] Violin accompanists necessarily imitate vocal rendering. Weighty music compositions and hundreds of devotional songs of the age of Bhakti are treasures of traditional knowledge and pointers to practice of Carnātic music. It is firmly believed that traditional forms preserve the authenticity of rāga forms and styles of rendering.

Introduction of the violin did stimulate musical activities. Music is communication and compositions are instruments of communication. Pronunciation of the text (Sāhitya) is the exclusive privilege of the vocalist. To know the meaning of the Sāhitya is as important for a dancer as to the instrumentalist and listener. The instrumentalist like the dancer is denied the privilege of spelling out the text. 'Creative part' (aspect) of rendering a composition is an excercise in effective communication. Musicians of the west realise it by exploiting ideas and forms. As Yehudi Menuhin stated "that particularly human phenomenon distilled to a rare potency—half tiger, half poet—the violinist is an incarnation of a specific animal agility in the service of a peculiarly human transfiguration. It is up to the violinist to speak of human memory, feeling or thought. The violinist makes such intangibles palpable by expressing them in sound and rhythm."

Carnātic music audience are accustomed to listen to the compositions of the 'Trinity' and others of their age. The conventional belief is that none will attempt to play or sing a number better than the composer himself since he knows how to interpret his creation best.[22] If this view is admitted it would mean that the composer should always be an expert exponent either a vocalist or an instrumentalist. In actual practice this is far from the truth. The adaptation of violin as a concert instrument proves that the conventional view is a truism.

About the adaptation and import of violin details are available to us. The instrument entered India during the time of Tipu Sultān of Mysore.[23] It must have become popular by A.D. 1850. The date of adoption of the instrument by Bāluswāmī Dīkṣitar is claimed to be A.D. 1805. Vaḍivelu Naṭṭuvanār (A.D. 1810 to 1847) popularised it among the Carnātic musicians. This adoption had served as a catalytic agent. Earliest attempts 'to compose for the violin' is said to be that of Muttuswāmī Dīkṣhītar. He has composed few pieces on the western model known as 'Nōṭṭu svarās'.[24] Varāhappa Iyer, Thanjāvur Subba Iyer and Tiruveṅkāḍu Śivarāmakṛṣṇa Iyer and others who lived during this time interval consolidated the attempt. The first violinist who attempted a solo performance is Tirukkoḍikkāval Kṛṣṇa Iyer (1857 to 1913 A.D.), Karūr Ċinnadēvudu alias Kṛṣṇayy (A.D. 1861 to 1901) and Malaikkōttai Gōvindaswāmī Piḷḷai are well-known violin maestros. Pudukkoṭṭai Nārāyaṇaswāmī Iyer, a contemporary of Gōvindaswāmī Piḷḷai (specialist in Rāgam, Tānam and Pallavī) composed the popular Pallavī 'Parimaḷa Renga Patē' usually rendered in the rāga Kāmbōti. Iluppūr Ponnuswāmī Piḷḷai, uncle of Tamil maestro Pançami and a close associate of Kaṅçirā maestro Mānmcoṇḍia Piḷḷai, composed Tillānas and Varṇas. Violin vidwan Annavarappu Rāmaswāmī had composed Kīrtanas Tillānas and Varṇas. Two rāgas Vaṇḍana (composition beginning with words Kanakāmbari) and Śrī Durgā (composition with the beginning Kanakadurgā Kvare) are his innovations. Violinist V.V. Subramanian is also a composer of merit having composed Kṛtīs. Tillānas and Bajan songs. He had ushered in rāgas like Priyarañjanī and Rādāpriya. He had also composed *Nōṭṭusvarās* full of harmonics and chords. M. Balamuralīkṛṣṇa, a reputed vocalist and a violin player has a large number of compositions to his credit. Lalgudi G. Jeyarāman, the violin maestro is the composer of quite a variety of Kīrtanas, Varṇas, and Tillānas. Of the earlier generation of violinists Karūr Cinnadēvudu and Daksiṇāmūrti Śāstrī have composed about thirty one Kīrtanas. The art of composition is neither learnt in a single day nor even the life-time of an individual. It is an age-long practice rather than a memory. The entry of violin had not called for special variety of compositions to enhance its own popularity.[26]

Mysore T. Chowdiah, the well-known violin maestro demonstrated that as many as two hundred and fifty six notes could be played by a single operation of (one way) bowing.[27] This was an innovative technique in violin play. In 1928 the Music Academy, Madras had resolved to ban seven stringed violin which Chowdiah was using. The maestro engaged Gokhale hall for an entire season to popularise the use of the seven stringed violin. He also reminded the public of the possibilities of using a twenty-one stringed violin and a single stringed violin. Triukkōdikkāval Krsṇa Iyer had already successfully demonstrated the possibility of playing a single stringed violin. T. Chowdiah composed number of Krtīs and Tillānas using the mudra (pen name) 'Tirumakūṭa'.[28] The innovations ushered in by Chowdiah are contributions to the technique of violin play. Sanskrit grammarians do affirm that ideas are conveyed through 'sounds' by a process of cognition' (Pratyabigyāna) and not by direct perception. By training, memory records a particular succession of sounds rather than another we may come to hear. In other words, compositions train us to get from the music 'a meaning—an expression'.

Violin it must be borne in mind had not altered the purpose or structure of compositions. The adoption kindled interest and innovations of techniques were brought. Kārvais' for instance could be made use of to make sound production faithful to the Sāhitya. 'Otukkal prayōgas' (scunding 'G' from the position of 'M' or 'D' from 'P') gliding gamakas and a rapid succession leading to anusvaras are all made use of. Reputed exponents have established several effective lines of transmission in style, technique and fidelity without encroaching on the traditional art of composing. Violin had been adopted to assist vocal style. Violin bow plays a vital role. The bowing technique plays an equally vital role. It spells each syllable of the Sāhitya. If the bow just dances on the 'svarastānas' alone this could not have been achieved. The 'Bhāva' aspect of any composition depends on the 'Dhātu' (Text). For example, the

Anupallavī of the popular Tyāgarāja number 'Sāmajavaragamana' what is often played is 'Sāmani-gamaja' which should be 'Sāma-nigamaja.[29] Violin maestros have successfully evolved a technique of bowing known as 'Sāhitya Vil'.

The seven stringed violin of Chowdiah is a noteworthy improvisation. He added three parallel strings fitted close to the second, third and fourth strings. They were tuned to the corresponding lower octaves.[30] The first string (G string) had to be left in isolation since to find a string thick enough to sound the lower octave of 'G' could not be thought of. While handling such an instrument (a) fingers are to be placed vertically on the double strings for each note exactly at the same spot to obtain perfect blending. (b) posture of sitting of an Indian violinist normally would result in a lateral finger-touch position only except perhaps on the lower scroll and off the finger-board.

The duty of a violinist is well defined by Yehudi Menuhin : "We must preserve and restore all those values we hold in trust and every art which brings dignity, nobility, and security to the human being. Music is the bridge between the abstract and the tangible, between imagination and reality." Indian violin maestros stood up to this expectation.

The progress made by drama (Nātakam) served as an accelerating force to the progress of music. Based on the quantum of music used, dramas could be classified as (a) the 'Nāṭaka' wherein the use of music is only incidental. Amidst speech and action few songs set in simple rāgas figure for the purpose of enhancing the dramatic effect (character/incident); (b) the 'Nṛtya-nāṭakas, wherein there is a preponderance of dance element the primary interest of the enactment centres round dance. They are akin to 'Dṛsya Kāvyas'; (c) The Gēya nātakas or opera intended for being sung and also meant for being enacted, have fine orchestral, choral and dance elements. There are also Géyaçaritrams which are sung and not acted. These are categorised as 'Sṛvya Kāvyas'. Gīta-gōvindam (Jeyadeva). Nandanārcaritram of Gopālakṛṣṇa Bhāratī and Nowkāçaritram of Tyāgarāja are good examples of Geyanātakas since the story is conveyed through the sequence of songs and dialogues in prose and verse.[31] *Rakti rāgas* find favourite use in operas and dance-dramas as they effectively express sentiments and afford much scope for exhaustive and descriptive treatment.

The reign of Vijayarāghava Nāyak (Tanjore 1633 to 1673 A.D.) witnessed progress of literature and music. This is evidenced by Caturdandīprakāsa, one of the standard lakṣaṇagrantas of Carnātic music, and the fascinating *Pada* compositions of Ksētrayya.

Dramatic art became popular in Tamil Nadu since the latter half of the eighteenth century. Many amateur organisations appeared.[32] The independence movement gave fillip to the growth of amateur and professional organisation since drama proved to be an effective tool of propaganda. Professional actors of yesteryears (latter half of the eighteenth century) used to commence the entertainment by 10 p.m. and the entertainment would last till dawn. Music had a prominent part to play in these marathon shows.[33] The dramas made profuse use of Purāṇic themes and this adoption meant the introduction of a large number of songs. Shri C. Kanniah is to be remembered in the context. He was the proprietor of the professional troupe Śrī Krṣṇa Vinōda Sabha. He invited Hussein Baksh from Lahore for preparing the stage. Yekai Shaṇmugam Piḷḷai was the music composer. His compositions were set to tune by Amarkavi, a Hindustānī musician. It is reported that renowned musicians (Carnātic) of the times Kāñcipuram Nāinā Piḷḷai, Madurai Ponnuswāmī Piḷḷai, T.N. Rājaratnam Piḷḷai, Tiruppāmbaram Swāmīnata Piḷḷai, Malaikkōṭṭai Govindaswāmī Piḷḷai, Pudukkōṭṭai Daksiṇāmūrty Piḷḷai, Marungāpuri Gōpālakrṣṇa Iyer and others attended the programmes.

Shri S.G. Kittappa is an unforgettable name. His brothers Subbiah and Chellappa were the disciples of Swāmī Śaṅkar Doss. Kiṭṭappa entered the field in 1911 at the tender age of five. He also came under the tutelage of Swāmī Śaṅkar Doss. Mysore T. Chowdiah, the violin maestro was a great admirer of Kiṭṭappa's music. It was Kittappa initiated the practice of introducing Kalpana svara bouts in drama platforms. Kittappa's golden voice (nay platinum voice) was so facile that he could handle any rāga with ease. K.B. Suṅdarambāḷ and M.S. Çelvāmbāḷ are well-known female artistes who rendered inestimable service for the propagation of Carnātic music on drama stages.

Resurgence of dramas received a setback with the advent of the films (cine industry). M.K. Tyāgarāja Bhāgavatar and many others acted in films and popularised Carnātic music. Pāpanāśam Śivan is a well-known composer who rendered yeoman service to

Carnātic music. Film-music was popular with the masses and they were initiated into listening to Carnātic music which was till then 'court and temple music'. Organising suitable songs to fit into the context was a challenging job and this required inclusion of Hindustānī, Carnātic and folk melodies. Borrowed elements were ornamented, coloured and stylised. The reasons for such metamorphosis are not far to seek : (a) Being a liberal art the sole aim is to colour the composition with extra-aesthetical elements. This lent the needed flexibility for weaving attractive melodic and rhythmic nuances. (b) A small number of artistes (gifted) dominated the field and compositions and tuning had to be designed to meet the demands of voice potential. (c) Choral music was in demand to supplement the stage-effects contemplated. (d) Use of unconventional percussion instruments influenced rhythm setting. (e) Orchestra which supplied supplemental melody consisted of a large number of instruments native and foreign. This necessitated changes in rhythmic structure. (f) Use of devotional songs by a choir included voices (male, female) of different pitch and intensity. Hand clapping was invariably retained, yet inclusion of varieties of musical instruments was inevitable. (g) The basics of rāgas are retained but the swarūpas (contours) necessarily get modified. (k) Compositions become tailored to meet the demands of sentiments and emotions. (l) Western influence in the shape of Rock, Jazz and Disco spread. (m) Songs are settled jointly by the composer, music-director, producer-director and the orchestral-director.

The result had been an abundance of music of more tonal colour, variety and finish. Some connoisseurs feel that the cumulative effect is to make music less tradition-bound. Film-music has such a mass appeal that it is intricately intertwined with socio-cultural scenario. It has become an essential component of 'Mass culture'. However, pioneer attempts at composing for the films are marked by better adherence to the 'classical version'.

The opening chapter of Bharata's work 'Nātyaśāstra' describes the process and evolution of 'Nāṭya Veda'. The creator meditates and the creative potential of the mind operates to bring forth the desired end-product.[34] The 'Fifth Veda' came into existence and from the elements of the four Vedas synthesised the 'Nāṭya Veda'.[35] Chapter seven of the 'Nāṭyaśāstra' deals with one hundred and eight tālas (Rhythmic varieties).[36] Aim of Nāṭya is to elaborate 'Rasa' while representing legends and themes drawn from Purāṇas. 'Nṛtta' added richness through rhythmic movements often to the accompaniment of music. The word 'Bharata' had traditionally received the interpretation 'Bha, Ra, Tha'—emotion (Bāva), Tune (Rāga) and Time measure (Tāla).[37]

In Tamil Nadu music and dance flourished, thanks to the support extended by the temples endowed by rulers. At Thanjāvūr (Tanjore), capital of the Chōlas, Nāyaks and Marāṭṭa princes, the arts flourished without interruption. The progress made during the Marāṭṭa rule may be briefly summarised. At the time of Marātta rulers dance art provided the motivation for music. To a music composer the most important requisite is not learning (Vyutpatti) or practice (Sādhanā) but 'Pratihbā' (originality and creative imagination). 'Pratibhā' is innate.[38] Composing demands a great deal of 'freedom'. It is the art of presenting musical thought in the form of something (subject). When we smell some unmistakable flavour or colouring in a composition we deem it 'romantic'. Those who composed for the dance art certainly realised this aspect. Vijaya-Rāgava Nāyak's rule (A.D. 1633 to 1673) is marked by a large output of Sāhitya and Saṅgīta. Marāṭṭa ruler Sahāji had left Laksaṇa grantas of great value. During Regunātha Nāyak's reign, dances have been performed pressing into use all the one hundred and eight tāla varieties. Some dance numbers were named after *Śūlāti Tālas* (Sūḷatinṛtta).[39] The Telugu work 'Rājagopāla Vilāsam' gives an elaborate picture of musical activities during the reign period of Regunāta Nāyaka and the early part of the reign of Vijayarāgava.[40] During the reign of Vijayarāgava Nāyaka 'Padas' and 'Yakṣagānas' become more popular.[41]

Compositions of Vijayarāgava Nāyaka for the enactment of Yaksagānas give us an idea of the conventions followed: (a) The usage of chosen rāgas at the commencement and conclusion of a play.[42] (b) The play 'Pūtanāharaṇam' makes use of rāgas like Kēdāragauḷa, Rēgupti, Śankarābharaṇam, Nilāmbari, Sāveri, Kāmbōji, Gaṇṭāravam, Jeyantaséna, Āhiri, Madyamāvati, Saurāṣtram, Bhūpāḷam, etc. These are used in 'Gollapātalu' and 'Darūs.'[43] (c) Aṭa Tāla (fourteen beats) is used in many Darūs.[44] This improvisation coincides with the opening of a new chapter in the history of style of music-writing.[45]

Sahāji the Marātta ruler is the author of many works which include drama, poetry, Prabhandas, and *Padās*. His *Pada* collections are well known (Tyāgēśa Padās, Padas in Marātti, Telugu and Sanskrit).[46] His *Gēyanātakas* (operas) usher in an era of fresh musical style. The triple arts of music, dance, and writing are fully exploited. Serfōji (1712 to 1728 A.D.) continued the patronage of arts and letters. Enacting of musical plays in temples continued. His successor Tuḷaja I (Tukkōji A.D. 1728 to 1736) is the author of the monumental work 'Saṅgīta Sārāmṛta'. These royal durbars of the southern princes patronised Hindustānī music too.[47] Nellore Śivarāma Kavi describes Tuḷaja as a liberal benefactor. (Kāmakalānidi) Eighteen Padās composed by Tuḷaja are preserved.[48] Some Padās contain Çiṭṭaswarās and Jatīs appended to them at the end of Anupallavī and Çaraṇa. They display influence of Maharāṣtra music.

Śivakāmasundarī Pariṇaya Nāṭakam opens with a 'Dvipada' which contains Darūs in the rāgas Nāthanāmakṛhya and Kāpi.[49] Emotions are conveyed through the 'Pravēśa Darūs' in the rāgas Kalyāṇī, Bairavī, Savēri, Rāmakṛya, Begada and other *rakti rāgas*. From internal evidences (Śivakāmasuṅdarī Pariṇaya Nāṭakam) it is known that the play was enacted in the temple of Āti Varāhaswāmī (Mahādēvapaṭṭiṇam).[50] A Sanskrit play 'Rājaranjana Vidyāvilāsa Nāṭakam' authored by Tuḷaja introduces Darūs, Dvipadas, Siramulu and other formats stimulating 'Moha' (Illusion). The rāga used is 'Mohanam' (Rēgupati). The pravēśa (entry) of the character 'Ānanda' (Joy/Mirth) is in the rāga Ānaṅdabairavī. When Lord Śaṅkara is portrayed as appearing on the stage the rāga Śaṅkarābaraṇam is used.

Stimulation of progress in music due to the growing popularity of dance-forms could be summarised. It resulted in the flowering of (a) Art-musical forms (Kṛti, Rāgamālika, Tānavarṇam) (b) Dance musical forms (Padam, Jāvaḷis Tillāna, Padavarṇam, Sabdam, Svarajatīs and Jatisvarā) (c) Technical and preparatory forms (Gīta, Sūḷati, Alaṅkāra and Prabhandā) (d) Devotional music forms mainly used in congregations and Harikatha performances (Taraṅgam, Utsava Sampradāya kīrtana, Aṣṭąpati, Ūñjal, Mangaḷam, etc.) (e) Opera forms for dance-drama and folk plays (Kuṛavaṅci, Yakṣagānam, Gēyaprabhandam, Lāvani, etc.). The contributors included (a) court musicians (Girirājakavi, Sōmakavi, Todī

Sītārāmayya, Śaṅkarābaraṇam Narasimha Ayya, Pallavī Doraiswāmī Iyer and others) (b) Recipients of royal patronage (Vīrabadrayya, Kavī Māṭrubūtaiyya, Maruttūr Kāsināta, Pallavī Gōpālayya and others) (c) Saint composers (Pedda Dāsari, St. Tyāgayya, Bhōtēndra Satguruswāmī, Sādāśiva Brahmēndra, Muttuttāṇḍavar and others) (d) musicians and professional composers (Paṭnam Subramania Iyer, Mahā Vaidyanāta Iyer, Subbarāma Dīkṣitar, Vīṇā Kuppier, Tiruvottiyūr Tyāga Iyer and others).

With increasing popularity of dance-dramas (Meḷanātakams in Tamil) innovative rhythmic varieties appeared.[51] Up-to the seventeenth century, compositions were noted for the excellence of the Sāhitya (text). 'Gatya Sāhityas' were now superceded by 'Metrical Sāhityas'. The 'Nāṭaka kīrtanas' (as those of Aruṇācalakavirāyar) include Viruttam and couplets (Iraṭṭaikkaṇṇikal as they are known in Tamil-Tipati). A 'Nāṭaka Kīrtanai' happily amalgamates Sāhitya (text), Music (tune), and Tāḷa (appropriate Gati). Thus it seeks to ensure perfect communication of the emotion which the performer is anxious to achieve. 'Laya Prastāra' (weaving of Tāḷa intricacies) are systematised and new varieties grow. These developed patterns guide composers who appear later.[52] Motivation provided by Bharatam and dance-dramas increased output of compositions which happily blended with the inevitable orchestral music.

Till a few decades ago the solo Bharatanātyam concert was known by the name 'Śadir'. A Śadir party with the dancing girl, nattuvanār, percussionist and other instrumentalist was called 'Cinna-mēḷam'.[53] Some varieties of compositions used in Śadir figure in present-day Bharatanāṭyam performances also. (Alārippu, Jatisvaram, Śabdam, Varṇam, Padam, Jāvali and Tillāna). These items are in circulation since the time of the Tanjore quartette (perhaps earlier) Çinniah, Ponniah Śivānandam and Vaḍivēlu. The brothers lived during the time of Serfōji II, the Marātta prince of Tanjore[54] (A.D. 1798 to 1832). They were also the hereditary Naṭṭuvāṅgam office holders of the Bṛhadeeśvar temple at Tanjore. 'Saṅgīta Muktāvali' a music treatise (late seventeenth century) describes the Lāsya type of dance that existed and mentions dance items such as Puṣpāñjalī, Śudda Yati, Śabda-sāli, Sūdāti, Sapta nṛttam, Sudā gīta Abinayam, Prabhanda nartanam, and Dṛvapādam. These varieties could have influenced the quartette.

Besides giving artistic touch to them they composed new varieties to enrich Bharatanātya repertoire which included Nṛtta, Nttya, and *Abinaya.* Before the time of the quartette, the performance had 'Mēḷaprāpti' to begin with which the *Naṭṭuvanaṛ* and the supporting orchestra rendered. The compositions were set in approved rāgas (constant) and tāḷas. This was followed by 'Tōḍayamaṅgaḷam' invoking divine blessing.[55]

'Alārippu' is an invocatory piece where the dancer offers his/ her obeisance to the Gods, Gurus, and the audience. Like the blossoming flower, the dancer's body and mind blossom to perform more exacting items scheduled. It is not set in any particular rāga or set of notes predetermined. The rhythmic syllables are spelt by the Naṭṭuvanār in the first, second and third speeds and end with a Jāti passage called 'Teermānam'.[56] Alārippu is set in tīśra, miśra, ċaturaśra, kaṇta and saṅkīrṇa naṭais. Jatisvaram has a string of notes set to a rāga and tāḷa. It is possible that this item could have originally been just a Jati sequence. Jatisvaram starts with a brisk Tīrmānam with the first svara passage performed in three or four varieties with a change in Naṭai in the last sequence of the first passage before shifting to the succeeding svara passage.

'Śabdam' has Sāhitya (text) and hence introduces Abhinaya. Normally it is in praise of God or a great patron of art. Conventionally, it consisted of four lines, every line being preceded by a short Jati sequence of 'Śolkaṭṭu'.[57] The rāga Kāmbōji and the tāḷa Çāpu have been much in favour, and yet it is sometimes tuned as a rāgamālika. The next item Padavarṇam (also known as Çhowkka varnam) is in a slower tempo when compared with rendering of a Tāna varṇam. Tānavarṇam has Sāhitya for Pallavī, Anupallavī and Çaraṇa whereas Padvarṇam has Sāhitya for the entire piece including Muktāyi and Eṭṭukkaḍai svaras. The opening line of Pallavī is preceded by 'Trikāla tīrmānam' followed by leisurely Abinaya. Rāga, Tāla and Bhāva get interwoven.

Padams are love lyrics, Śṛṅgāra padās scoring high in popularity.[58] A Jāvaḷi is lighter in vein and more lively. The attractive rhythm in Dēśāti, or *Madhyāti* tālas and the captivating music make it charming and inviting. Tillānas are set in solfa syllables and end with a small line of *Sāhitya. Tillāna* helps the nṛtta aspect since Sāhitya content is minimum. Introduction of cross rhythms (Natai) adds beauty to the composition. The popularity of Tillānas is due to the fact that (a) Solfa syllables Ta, Ka, Ta, Ri, Ki, Ta, Na, Ka are used, (b) Familiar syllables are made use of, (c) the Sāhitya is used sparingly and crisply. The 'Śolkattu' is a feature of early Prabhaṅdas referred to as 'Pāṭam'. Medieval Prabhaṅdas have a section called 'Pātava Khaṇḍa'.

To begin with compositions were panegyric addressed either to a king or a personal deity. In the next stage, in their metrical forms, a composition found spontaneous expression of love, jealousy, sorrow or valour. In spite of the emotional content and appealing music rendition, these extempore improvisations were defective in literary sophistication and commanded little or no recognition by scholars of erudite society as far as the verbal form was concerned. But the lilt in the rhythmic patterns and the soulful melody fascinated and found ready response in the creative fountain and reservoir of devotional lyrics and lyrical plays of Purāṇic themes. Then appeared the 'Mārgā literature' (Kāvyas) of royal courts. In an opera or music dance-drama the emotional presentation does not get evenly distributed throughout the play. Incidental songs in 'Veetinātakams', *Bāgavēta mēḷa, Yakṣagāna*, were set to tunes after composition of texts. Motivations however had resulted in a fruitful harvest of variety of music compositions.

What is regarded as traditional Bharatanāṭyam today reflects the model laid down by Sadir.[59] "The infusion of creative energy marks the early nineteenth century as one of the most innovative periods in the history of Indian dance."[60] Some of the dance-compositions which have developed (since the dance moved away from the temples) have been rechoreographed. The new material is loosely associated with the earlier temple tradition. Ashok Ranade's observation is to be quoted in the context. "The truth is that music does not become devotional because its maker was/is in a devotional frame of mind while making it."[61] Numerous historical references linking courtesans with music and dance suggest that the secular component was always strong. The fillip gained a pleasing variety and range of choice to the artistes.

Some of the technical terms demand brief note for proper understanding of the structures themselves. 'Jatisvaram' denotes a musical composition which is sung with svaras only and Svarajati is a composition with svara phrases and fitting Sāhitya. Many of the Prabhadas mentioned by Mataṅga, Sārṅgadeva, and others had *svaras* and *Hastapātas* (syllabic sounds of musical instruments) as inherent features. The *Dvipada Prabhandas* were composed with *svaras* only. The *Vādya Prabhandas* and *Nṛtya Prabhandas* (instrumental and dance forms) may be said to be forerunners of compositions without regular Sāhitya like Jatisvaram. Jatisvaram was also known as 'Svara Pallavī'.[62] A less known composer of Andhra Pradesh Vasa Appayya (first half of the eighteenth century) had composed Svarapallavis mostly intended for practice on vīṇā. Musical forms without words using svaras and Jatis called 'Jatisvarams' came into vogue during the nineteenth century. The earliest available Jatisvarams may be said to be those of the Tanjore quartette. At the initial stages there seems to have been a profusion of Jatis which with efflux of time have been replaced by solfa syllables and as a result the Jatisvaram now in vogue must have been born. We are unable to determine the authors of many of the Jatisvarams available in chronologically earlier publications in Telugu (Svaramañjarī of Taççūr Śṛṅgārāçāri, Saṅgīta Vidyā Bhōdini, Gandharva Karpavalli, etc.). It appears 'Svarajati' and 'Jatisvaram' have been used to designate one and the same variety.[63]

As an item of dance 'Svarajati' has svara passages and fitting Sāhitya. Melattūr Vīrabadrayya happens to be the earliest composer of this variety. Tanjore quartette have also composed Svarajatis and they are more in the model of Padavarnas. Sāhitya part in Pallavī and Anupallavī are minimum, there is elongation of vowel sounds as in Varṇas and the Muktāyi svara sāhitya is intercepted with Jatīs. The Gānakrama is also like that of a varṇa with two separate sections one with Pallavī, Anupallavī, and Muktāyi svara and the second with Çaraṇa and Ettukkaṭai svaras. There are svarajatīs in Telugu, Tamil and Sanskrit. Śṛṅgāra is the favourite theme though the Bhakti element is dominant in some Svarajatīs. Svarajatīs and Jatisvarams serve as 'Abhyāsa gāna' (practice in initiation of music).

Folk-melodies have also served as incentives to the increase of dance repertoire. *Kuṛavançi* is one of the varieties of folk dance.[64] This is said to be an evolved pattern of the *Kuluva* dance depicting the unsophisticated amours of the *Kurava folk*. To this nucleus was later added the theme of a damsel falling in love with the deity of the region and pining for union with him. The heroine has a confidant (Sakhi) who serves as the love messenger. The male and female *Kuṛavas* are termed as '*Siṅgan*' and '*Siṅgī*'. *Siṅgi*, true to the tribe's pretensions to fortune telling, reads the palm of the heroine and predicts union. The jealous Siṅgan who goes in search of his spouse reprimands the spouse for her absence from the house and their quarrel affords a humourous interlude. The verses in the Kuravanci are in Āśiriyappā, Sindu and Kaṇṇi metres. 'Kuṛavāñci' was normally enacted in the temples. Tirukkuṟṟāla Kuṛavañci, Ardhanāreeśvara Kuṛavañci and Tiruvārūr Kuṛavañci are some well-known examples. To please kings and chieftains they were introduced as Nāyakās. The Śarabhēndrabhūpāla Kuravañci is an outstanding example. Several such Kuṛavañcis were composed to honour Maṟava and Kaḷḷar chieftains who lived in the sixteenth, seventeenth and eighteenth centuries.[65]

Lāvaṇi singing becomes popular at Thanjāvūr during the rule of the Marāṭtas (A.D. 1684 to 1855). This ballad-like composition (Lāvaṇi) is claimed to have been born at Maharāṣtra. The last Marāṭṭa ruler Sivāji II (Tanjore) was a lover of Lāvaṇis. He is the hero of some of the Lāvaṇi compositions. Lāvaṇi Venkata Rao is an expert Lāvaṇi exponent who adorned the court of Sivāji II.[66] The composition adopts a format, wherein number of puzzles are raised and answers are provided. The puzzles are based on Purāṇic incidents and sacred literature. 'Lāvaṇi' means 'an offshoot' and refers to extempore music on the spot. In the Tamil language it is designated as 'Nilāvaṇi'. Lāvaṇi is rendered by a troupe in chorus. The leader of each group (Sahir) is a talented musician and poet who can compose on the spot and provide the appropriate tune too. (Āśukavitvam) All the nine rasas are effectively portrayed and stimulated. Of the many troupes of Lāvaṇi singers, some were devotees of Śiva and others of Viṣṇu. When the troupes enter into a debate, it will produce a thrilling experience to the listeners.[67] Lāvaṇis in the Marātti language are lengthy pieces with a refrain (Dṛvapadā) which is analogous to the Pallavī and is followed by many caraṇas. Music of Dṛvapada is repeated as in the rendering of Aṣṭapati hymns at the completion of every stanza. Çaraṇas too have identical musical settings. Marātti Lāvaṇis were originally sung in the rāga 'Kāpi' (Carnātic). Later, sophisticated tuning involved use of attractive rāgas and tālas. Lāvaṇīs were composed in the Tamil language too. Kannada Lāvaṇis were equally popular. 'Tuṅtina' and 'Deph' provided the drone and rhythmic background.

Samarta Rāmdoss the preceptor of Çhatrapati Śivāji is the earliest known composer of Lāvaṇis. Tukāram, Éknāth, Ānandapanti, Mādhava-muni and Amṛta Rai have composed Lāvaṇis which are popular unto this day. Parasurām Ēsu rendered the great epic Mahābarata in Lāvaṇi verses. On the basis of the content, the Lāvaṇis are classified as: (a) Śṛṅgāra Lāvaṇis (b) Note Lāvaṇis (Salute Lāvaṇi) (c) Samvatsara Lāvaṇi (d) Bārakāti Lāvaṇis (e) Pançabāṣa Lāvaṇis (f) Vedānta Lāvaṇis (g) Conversational Lāvaṇis, (for example, Śiva-Pārvatī Samvāda, Nārada Samvāda, Suka-Ramba Samvāda, etc.) (h) Lāvaṇis in praise of Iṣṭa devatās (personal deities) (i) Lāvaṇis praising the Bhaktas (devotees) (j) Pālna Lāvaṇis (Cradle songs) (k) Lavāṇis on Purāṅic themes (Rāmāyaṇa Lāvaṇi, Bāgavata Lāvaṇi Daśāvatāra Lāvaṇi, etc.) (l) Subadrākalyāṇa Lāvaṇi (m) Advaita Lāvaṇi (n) Tīrta yātra Lāvaṇi (o) Lāvaṇis in praise of patrons (The Rāgamālika Lāvaṇi during the time of king Serfōji II praises him). It is in classical mode making use of rāgas like Sāveri, Kānada, Dhanyāṣi, and Śrī rāga) (p) Nowkā Lāvaṇi (deals with the boyhood pranks of Lord Kṛṣṇa. St. Tyāgarāja chose the theme 'Nowkā Krīta' or Kṛṣṇa's play in the boat sailing, in his opera 'Nowkā-çaritram'. Kavi Veṅkaṭasūri later in point of time to Tyāgarāja produced a 'Nowkā Çaritra' in Sanskrit. A Lāvaṇi, popularly known as 'Nowkā' was composed in Marātti and this is a typical ballad. Having a lilting rhythm this ballad is attractive and when rendered accompanied by Tuntina and Deph the rural charm it provides is irresistible. (q) Lāvaṇīs dealing with sublime divine themes were composed by Tukāram, Nāmdéva, Rām Jōṣi and others.

Lāvaṇīs in Tamil were composed in large numbers. They are very popular with the rural folk. During the Tamil calendar month of Māṣi (February-March) the advent of Spring would be announced with gay and mirth. A festival by name 'Kāman Paṇḍikai' would be observed. Lāvaṇi debates during such festivals are invariably arranged. Two troupes participate taking opposite sides and the argument would centre round the question whether Maṅmata was burnt to ashes by Lord Śiva? The opposition troupe will argue in favour of taking 'Manmata Dahana' as an allegory and that Cupid is never dead once the 'carnal desire' (Kāma) is extinguished. References to Purāṇic incidents, allusions and comparisons are used in profusion and the combat is a musical discussion. The performance will last till dawn and after the event a Maṅmata's effigy is burnt. These on the spot compositions constitute an attractive part of the musical heritage of Tamil Nadu.

An opera enacted by men (Bhāgavata méḷa) of the Brahmin community has its origin at Melāṭṭūr near Thanjāvūr. Popularly known as Bhāgavata mēḷa it has a religious tinge. Inspired by Nārāyaṇa Tīrta's 'Kṛṣṇalīlātaraṅgiṇi' and the Yakṣagāna play 'Pārijāta apaharaṇam', Veṅkaṭarāma Bhāgavatar of Mēlāṭṭūr an elder contemporary of St. Tyāgarāja composed in Telugu twelve opera plays based on Purānic themes and enacted them in the local temple. Bālu Bhāgavatar of Śūlamaṅgalam, an adjoining village is another exponent of this variety of art. Customarily these are enacted in the month of Vaisākha (May-June) in some villages of Tanjore such as Mālāṭṭūr, Śūlamaṅgalam and Śāliyamaṅgalam. It is remarkable that these male artistes exhibit all the charms in abhinaya (female artistes claim monopoly in this aspect) foot movements and flexures. They wear appropriate masks and enact plays on an improvised stage where the actors and supporting musicians move about all the time before an appreciative audience.

The marionette show known as 'Bommalāṭṭam' is another refined folk entertainment. Suitable decorated dolls are made to dance. The movements are manipulated from behind the scene by experts in the craft with the help of black strings. To music played in the classical mode, the dolls dance items like Alārippu, Jatisvaram and Tillāna. Bommalāṭṭam was patronised by the Nāyak rulers of Tanjore. Nāṇu Iyengar was a great exponent and Vīrakavirāyar wrote short plays specially for Nāṇu Iyengar. The 'Puravi āṭṭam' (Poikkāl kutirai or Dummy horse show) is a familiar entertainment in festivals. A horse made of bamboo framework pasted over with paper and cardboard painted and saddled has a split in its body big enough for a man to stand in and manipulate activities of a driver. His feet rest on short stilts and the body above the waist can be seen. The dances on stilts go on to the accompaniment of Nādasvaram capering and gyrating in alternatively slow or quick tempo.

A vigorous dance by a group of fifteen or twenty men is the 'Oyilāṭṭam'. The performers are trained by an experienced elder who captains the team clad in gaudy coloured breeches and shirts with ankle bells and shoulder scarf and bearing staffs they move vigorously in a circle waving coloured towels. The leader starts the song which the others repeat in chorus dancing with simple step movements. Oyilāṭṭam in temples have for their themes the wedding of Vaḷḷi, episodes from the Purāṇas or exploits of local deities. Elsewhere the theme is martial and narrates exploits of chiefs. The dance songs are in Sindu or Kaṇṇi metre. Vaḷandān is another martial composition rendered in group dance. The 'Anbunāṭṭu Vaḷandān' popular in Pudukkōṭṭai region of Tamil Nadu praise the members of the Toṇḍaimān royal house. 'Kuḷuval' is another variety. They are popular in Tiruççirapaḷḷi, Madurai and Rāmanāthapuram districts, the homeland of Maravā and Kaḷḷar chieftains. In the Coimbatore district Purāṇic themes are popular. 'Çākkai āṭṭam' once popular in parts of Tānjore and Tiruççirapaḷḷi districts was in praise of Murukan, Māriamman and other deities. The dancing performers manipulate four short sticks mostly strung in a thread and held between fingers.

Çindūs (melodies) are compositions which incorporate folk-forms like Temmāngu. Compositions of this type produced by Seeni Āçāri (1852 to 1902) are said to be the earliest. In the compositions of Seeni Āçāri amorous themes predominate. Another contemporary composer of Kāvaṭi Çindu is Uttaṇḍam Piḷḷai of Karivaḷam vanta nallūr. (Tirunelveli district) Compositions of the same variety having Islamic themes as content are known as 'Poovaṭi Çindu'. These have been composed by Asan Ali of Mēḷappāḷayam (Tirune veli district).

By far the most known composer of Kāvaṭi Çindūs is Çennikuḷam Aṇṇāmalai Reddiyar (A.D. 1865 to 1891). It is said that Ponnammāḷ of Karivalamvanta nallūr helped Reddiyar to set tunes to his compositions and print them with suitable notations.[68] Melody is captivating and appeals to mass and class. Vīṇā brothers Kāraikuḍi Sāmbaśiva Iyer and Subbarāma Iyer, Maḷavārayanēndal Subbarāma Bāgavatar, Harikēśvanallūr Mutthia Bhāgavatar, and Tiruççendūr Ṣaṇmugavaḍivu are some of the well-known exponents of Kāvaṭi-Çindu.

Musical forms owe their origin to the medieval Prabhandas. 'Prabhanda' is a generic term which refers to any well-knit composition, but in music it is a particular form where there are several varieties adhering to the prescribed norms. Matanga's Bṛhaddeśī makes mention of Prabhanda for the first time and it receives a comprehensive treatment at the hands of Śārngadeva. (Sangīta Ratnākaram) Prabhandas are broadly classified as Sūḍa,

Aḷi and Viprakīrṇa. Sūḍaprabhanda is of two kinds—Suddha-Sūḍa and Sāḷagā Sūḍa. Sāḷaga Sūḍa is of seven types: Dṛva, Mattapratimatta, Nisa Adda, Rasa, and Ekatāli, Dṛuva Prabhanda is the progenitor of the musical form 'Dāru'.

Bharata in his work Nāṭyaśāstra devotes an entire chapter to Dṛuva songs (stage songs) illustrating different varieties. They are versified musical compositions which form an important part of the early Sanskrit dramas. Many of these Dṛuva songs bear a close resemblance to some of the 'Darūs' of post-medieval operas and dançe dramas.[69] Different classes of Dṛuva prabhandams are dealt with by Regunāta Nāyaka in his lakṣaṇa treatise 'Saṅgīta Sūḍa' Darū figures in Yakṣagāna.[70] Darūs gain wide currency and popularity in the Nāṭya and Gēya nāṭakas composed during the ruie of the Marātta princes of Tanjore.

Darūs have been classified according to the purpose they served. 'Swāgata Daru' denotes musical soliloquy with a melody of a recollective nature. 'Pralāpa Daru' portrays sorrow; Heççarika Darū is for saluting a monarch and Padavaṅdana-Darū refers to approaching the sanctum of a deity.

Number of Darūs were composed for musical plays enacted at the royal courts. Such are the 'Tenṭral Darū', 'Vennilā Darū', 'Maṅmata Darū', etc., dealing especially with the experience of courtesans in love with the hero who was invariably the king. These Darūs on love themes may be considered as forerunners of Jāvaḷi.[71] Jāvaḷis are mostly in Rakti rāgas. Along with its characteristic tempo, they bring out an amorous theme. Like the Kāvaṭi Çindu, Jāvāḷi shows how the creative power of music was active in projecting new and delightful forms. The very name 'Jāvali' is intriguing. Kittel's Kannada dictionary notes Jāvaḷi as a variety of lewd poetry. It is not a Marātti word. Tamil Lexicon (3874) mentions Jāvali as a derivation of 'Jhwāli:' stated to be a Urdu word. Persian and Urdu scholars do not approve of this derivation. It is not a 'Dēśi musical number'. Some Sanskrit scholars connect it with Capala. Telugu dictionaries of the last quarter of the last century note the word. Jāvaḷi composers belong to the last quarter of the last century. Hence it is difficult to judge the indebtedness of Jāvaḷi to Darūs.

Kings Sahāji and Tulajāji perfected the Darū forms. Tradition of literary Prabhandas and Yaksagānas were combined.[72] Special types of Darūs composed by Sahāji are 'Salām Darū' and 'Jakkiṇi Darū' and they belong to Dēśī music. Jakkiṇi Darūs are deemed to be the forerunners of Tillāna. The 'Mātu' of the first section of the Jakkiṇi Darū consists entirely of Jatis while the text 'Dhātu' figures in the second part.[73] Sage Mataṅga is claimed to be the pioneer in Jakkiṇi dance. Jakkiṇi Darūs are traced to Jakkuḷas a section of dancers from Andhra Pradesh and artistes who played a variety of drum called Jakki.[74] Kuṛavançi nāṭakas like 'Tyāgēśa Kuṛavançi' contain number of Jakkiṇi Darūs.

'Varṇana Darū' as the name suggests and describes the personality of the king, place, incident, background, etc. 'Samvāda Darū' denotes a musical dialogue or conversation between two characters with the presumption that the conclusion is foregone.[75] Tuḷajāji's opera 'Rājamaṅjana Vidyā Vilāsa' abounds in ragas like Mōhanam (illusion) indicating particular moods. Ghanaśyāma is the author of an allegorical drama by name 'Navagrahaçaritra' which contains Pātrapravēśa Darūs. Kavi Mātrubhūtayya's Yakṣagāna 'Pārijātapaharaṇa Nāṭakamu' contains Maṇipravāḷa Darūs (mixture of Hindi, Marātti, Telugu and Tamil). In Girirājakavi's (court poet of Serfōji) work 'Rājamohana Kuṛavaṅçi' the heroine sends two messages to the king through a parrot. The messages are Darū compositions and tuned in the rāga Bairavī. A Pravēśa Darū indicates the advent of the Kuṛavaṅçi and the happy union of the couple is predicted by reading the heroine's palm.

The Rāmanāṭakam of Aruṇāçalakavi contains about two hundred Darūs. The compositions have multiple çaranas and they are usually rendered in slow tempo. (Viḷamba kāla) These Darūs feature have many proverbs.[76] King Sahāji had composed 'Anulōma Vilōma Darūs'.[77] Rāmaswāmī Dīksitar (father of Muttuswāmī Dīkṣitar) composed similar Darūs in Sanskrit.[78] The 'Koṇaṅki Darū' is rendered when the divine clown appears. The Bhāgavatamēḷa Naṭakams of Melāṭṭūr Veṅkaṭaramaṇa contain many Darū variety of compositions.[79] Rāga Kāmbōji is the favourite choice for rendering the Darūs and the tessera often hovers round Tāra Ṣadja. Composition of Darūs have been favoured by post-Trinity composers too.

Anecdotes culled out of the Purāṇas constitute a common thread of all performing arts. The skill acquired in performing, marks the individuality of each production. The Marātta rulers of Thaṅjāvūr invited 'Kīrtanakārs' from Gwalior and Pune and their performances became popular in Tamil areas.[80] 'Kīrtan' is a short metrical form of composition. This greatly aids Harikatha performances as they help the construction of the theme step by step. With the growing popularity of Harikatha performances in Tamil Nadu the need arose for composing specifically for the purpose and these compositions were modelled after Marātta Kīrtan.[81] A Harikatha performance is made up of narrative and music interwoven. (Nirūpana) The music has an important role to play since the narration includes verses taken from Purāṇas and epics. Varieties of compositions took shape such as Śāki, Diṇdi, Abhaṅg, etc. The different stages of the built-up content came to be accommodated in songs. The narrative portions were explanatory, explaining the meaning of the songs and the songs were tuned in classical, light-classical and folk-melodies. The compositions were metrical and extracts from Sanskrit and vernacular texts. Tradition-bound rāgas and tunes are made use of. Harikatha performers are composers of merit. The great contribution of Harikatha to Carnātic music is the variety of musical forms in different languages and varnameṭṭūs (tunes) based on Carnātic and Hindustānī modes. Harikathā Kālakṣēpams were indeed powerful catalytic agents.[82]

Devotional music had shaped and sustained the wider music culture of the country. The Āḷvārs and Nāyanmārs of the south, Vaiṣṇavite saints of the north—all chose the vehicle of music to sing the praise of the Lord. The general name given to devotional singing is 'kīrtana'. South India has evolved a rich and varied tradition which may be termed as 'Bhāgvata tradition'. It is cast in the classical mould of Carnātic music and in addition it has assimilated some of the best folk-melodies and elements from Kīrtana tradition of the north. The tradition is a great reconciler between classes and masses, between the north and the south. Tallappākkam Çinnayya (fifteenth century A.D.) is the founder of the 'Bhajana Paddati'. Jeyadēva, Çaitanya, Puraṅdaradāsa, Badrāçalam Rāmadāsa, Nārāyaṇa Tīrta, Sadāśiva Brahmēṅdra, Bodēṅdra Swāmī, Śrīdhara Ayyāvāl, and Sadguruswāmī are well-known Bhāgavatars. St. Tyāgarāja inherited the tradition. He converted a mere 'Gāyaka' (singer) into a 'Bhāgavata' (devotional singer). Concert music of the concert hall may be described as 'sophisticated Bhāgavata music.'

Proceedings in a congregation (Bhajanai) start with 'Puṇḍarīkam' chanted in unison with 'ādhāra śṛuti' (basic tonic) initiated by the leader and taken up by the congregation. 'Nāmāvalīs' (garland of the Lord's name) follow and these are exercises in rāga elaboration. Melody is the primary consideration; the cross-rhythmic play on the Mṛdaṅgam, Jālras, and Çiplās providing a highly pleasing musical effect. In the most sophisticated 'Pallavīs' of the concert platform we hear an extension of this set up. Then there are ślōkas elaborated in rāgas. Aṣṭapatis of Jeyadeva, Taraṅgiṇis of Nārāyaṇa Tīrta, compositions of Tyāgarāja, Puraṅdaradāsa, Bhadrāçalam Rāmadāsa, Gōpālakrṣna Bhāratī, Abaṅgs of Tukāram and the bhajans of Tulsī, Kabir, and Mīrābāī follow the artistic arrangements of ślōkas, song and nāmāvali following each other being kept up as far as possible. The famous Gopikāgītam from the Bhāgavata embodying Rāsalīlā is also sung. The yearning of the individual soul for union with the oversoul is best expressed in the form of Nāyaka-Nāyaki Bhāva.

Bhāgavata tradition in its various forms (Bhajan, Nāṭyanātakam, Bāgavata mēḷam, and Harikathā Kālakṣēpam) could be taken as the direct method in musical education.

Explanation, explication, understanding, analysis, explaining a work on the basis of the norms of the genre that represents, explicating the material content embodied in the work, understanding the composer behind the work and analysing the links that bind the various parts of the work—all these correspond to the different principles that for the past twenty-five years (sometimes claimed as 'modern age') have given music its meaning and established it as an art form. These principles, it is good to remember are not mutually exclusive, but replace each other as the prevailing view of their respective ages. The eighteenth-nineteenth centuries accorded special emphasis to the personal element of understanding a composer. It does mean that the actual poetic element of music, that quality by which music stands or falls as an art-form was sought in the originality with which a composer expressed his feelings and proving himself equal to the paradoxical task of making us sense the 'indescribable and ineffaceable'.

REFERENCES

1. A Gaelic myth states that it was precisely by opposing these three powers that King Leevellyn won legitimacy. The Tamil epic Śilappatikāram and anthologies of the Saṅgam Age give examples of music in war such as Munterkuravai, Pintér kuravai, etc.
2. *Dictionary of Music.* (Harvard University)
   F. Chrysander : Jahrbucher Fur musikakische. Wissenscheft (1863)
   Walde S. Pratt : On behalf of Musicology. (O. Thompson, International Encyclopaedia of Music and Musicians, 1839)
   H. Lang L. Harp : On the Nature of Musicology (Music Quarterly, XXIII).
3. Mataṅga is placed in the 9th century A.D. Mataṅga is the only link between Bharata and Abinavagupta. P.V. Kane places him in A.D. 750.
   V. Raghavan : Saṅgītha Nāṭaka Academy Bulletin, No. 5.
4. Tatā ca āha Bharatamuni : "Jāti Sambutatvāt, grāmarāgānām iti.
   Yati Kiṅcit gēyatē lōkē tatsarvam jātiṣu ateetam.
   Because grāma rāgas are born of Jātis whatever is sung in the world all that subsists in Jātis.
5. The work must have been composed in A.D. 1546. The author mentions Jam Sattrasal of Navanagar, Saurāṣtra (A.D. 1569 to 1608) as his patron. But he is silent about Śārṅgadeva, author of Saṅgīta-ratnākaram even though his indebtedness to Śārṅgadeva is obvious.
6. The author of Gaekwad Oriental Series, A.N. Jane observes that Rāmamātya's influence is traceable. But he attests that Puṇdarika Viṭṭala is Śrīkaṇṭha's preceptor. On this statement it is claimed that Śrīkaṇṭha hails from Karnātaka.
7. Śārṅgadeva speaks of twelve. Rāmāmātya says that trained ears must locate in subtle sounds of Aṅtara and Kākaḷi on the frets allocated to Rudra Vīṇā and 'Pa, Da, Pa'.
8. "Ṣadja ēva grāha: sarvarāgeṣu parikīrtita: (Rasakaumudi I. 83).
9. Saṅgita Ratnākaram: Verses 69 to 87.
10. The only parallel is available in Rāgaviboda of Somanāta, chronologically a later work.
11. "Dhyānam vīṇā Rāgasamūhamedam
    ... Saṅgīta śāstrōkta palayasya siddayē//
12. Most of these could be noted in the 'Prakīrṇa' chapter of Saṅgīta-ratnākaram. Śrīkaṇtha expresses different views about Śarira, pitfalls of Vākgēyakāras, etc. He concurs, largely with others.
13. There is a tendency to study terms by finding parallels in the English language. Primary sources do not get the attention they deserve. For example, Samvāda = consonance; Madyamā = fourth F; Sudda

= Neutral. The spirit of Sanskrit usage is lost when parallels are attempted. At times they even mislead.

14. Some of these may have historical leanings as for example 'the development of musical scales'. H. Weyal remarked "Mathematics may well be a creative activity of man like music, the production of which not only in form but also in substance is conditioned by the decisions of history and therefore defy complete objective rationalisation."

15. When we say Rāga Mohanam has five notes one can land at five points of measurable pitch.

    Abraham Paṇḍitar: Karṇāmṛtasāgaram. (Thanjavūr 1924).

16. B.C. Deva : The Vibrato in Indian music.

    Deva makes a meaningful suggestion that Gamakas of Indian music bear the burden of unconscious forces and the Vibrato is ruled out as unpleasant.

17. The stringed instrument Yāl provided the accompaniment. In the West Jerome of Moravia produced a Latin treatise (125 A.D.). He describes Viella as a 'bowed instrument of weighted body with five strings tuned to D, G, g, d, for *Secular Music*.

18. Many rāgas currently heard are innovations of later day musicians.

19. Vide Supra, Chapter III.

20. V. Rāghavan: Indian origin of the Violin. (*Journal of the Music Academy*, Madras, 1987).

21. Śārṁgadeva's Saṅgītaratnākara describes the bow in detail. (Ślōkas 402 to 411). The modern violin bow is indebted for perfection to the labour of Francois Tourte (A.D. 1750 to 1835) whose design is so final that no improvement has been possible.

22. It must however be admitted that documentation is poor.

23. Tipu Sultan could have noticed the instrument used by the French. The French deemed education in violin-play as an important requisite of building personality. It is well known that Tipu had a large number of French generals in his army.

24. There are about forty Nōṭṭusvaras in the Śanahrabharana rāga alone. Pattaṇam Subramaṇia Iyer (1848 to 1902 A.D.) in the Katanakutūhalam piece shows Western influence. Some of the Nōṭṭusvara composers are (a) Muttuswāmī Dīkṣitar (b) Garbhapuri Çinnadēvuḍu (c) Karūr Śivarāmiah (d) Thenmatam Narasimhaçārulu (e) Tiruppanandāḷ Paṭṭābhirāmiah.

25. Ponnuswāmī Piḷḷai's playing on the violin was laya oriented (Tālam). Notes like Ri, Ga, Ma he recognised as Ta-Ki-Ta and Ga, Ma, Pa, Da as Ta-ka-di-mi. He accompanied the veteran vocalist Kāñçipuram Nāina Piḷḷai. (This information was provided by the violin maestro late Kumbakoṇam Rājamāṇickam Piḷḷai).

26. Supra ; Chapter I.

27. This demonstration was at the Music Academy Conference at Madras in 1957.
28. The university of Mysore had brought out a book containing Chowdiah's compositions. The publication is edited by Prof. V. Rāmaratnam.
29. This composition of Tyāgarāja of Tiruvaiyāru is in the rāga Hiṅdōḷam set to Āti tāḷa. (Eight beats).
30. Similar experiments have been tried. Sadkāla Gōvinda Mārār used a Tamburin with seven strings. Gōṭṭuvādyam Sakārāma Rao used twelve strings. (Sympathetic). Palladam Sanjiva Rao used a flute with nine holes. Credit is due to Chowḍiah since he tried the experiment on an imported instrument.
31. P. Sāmbamurthy had edited Nowkāçaritram providing notation for songs with critical and explanatory notes. (Madras, 1962).
32. Suguṇa Vilāsa Sabhā was organised in 1891 A.D. at Madras. Doctors, lawyers, judges, professional engineers and others became members of the Sabha. Sir. C.P. Rāmaswāmī Iyer, R.K. Shanmugam Chettiar and such other celebrities were initiated by Pammal P. Sambanda Mudaliar. In 1914, Saśi Vilāsa Sabha appeared with Sir. C.P. Ramaswāmi Iyer as its president.
33. Subbarāyaçāri disciple of Appāvo Piḷḷai of Bangalore is one such professional.

    Pammal P. Sambandamudaliar: Nātakaṭ Tamil. (Madras, 1962), p. 82.
34. "Kirtanīyaka miççāmō ......

    Pañçamam sarvavaṃikam. (Ch. V. I.7)

    "Dharma mārtyam yakṣāsyam ça ......

    Caturvedāṅgā saṁbavam" (Ch. I. V.9)
35. "Jagrah patya mrgavēdat ......

    ...... Rasanadrva nādapi (Ch. I. V. 10)

    It included six sciences — details of sculptural art, architecture, drawing, playing instruments.
36. Śollukkattūs used in Bharatam are of very ancient origin.
37. Bakāro Bāvaityukta ; Ragarō Rāgaityuçyatē ; Takārō tāḷasamgyasça ityē vam Bharatam vitu:

    'Bharata Śenāpatīyam' a Tamil work repeats the same idea. Vedānta Dēśikan refers to it in his plays 'Saṅkalpa Sūryodayam' and 'Hastagiri māhātmyam'. Tiruvilayāṭal Purāṇam of Śēkkilar reflects the same view 'Bāvamōḍu rāga tāḷam immūnrum pakarntitum muṟṟiyal Bharatam"
38. Daṅḍin: Kāvyādarśa. I 103.
39. Regunātābhyudayam: Sarga 12. Ślōkas 26 to 29.

    (Mannar Serfoji Saraswatī Mahāl Library, Thanjavur).
40. Seṅgalvakalā kavi is an esteemed poet of the Tanjore court. (M.S.S.M. Library, Tanjore) (Series No. 33, 1951).

41. Yakṣagānas are musical plays. Many rāgas are used in compositions included in them. Some such usages provide the clue for tracing the history of rāgas of the Carnātic system. Musical instruments in use and a variety of compositions are also known from Yaksagāna texts.
42. Prahlāda Çaritram. (Andhra University Series, No. 55, 1955) Rāga Saurāstra is used at the commencement of the play. In Reghunātābyudayam this rāga is used at the beginning and at the end of the play. (Mangaḷa ślōka) St. Tyāgarāja employed Saurāstra at the commencement of his opera 'Prahlāda Bhakti Vijayam.'
43. Rāga Mohanam is not mentioned by that name. Some musicologists have identified Rēgupti with Mohanam.

    Ref: Pūtanāpaharaṇam. (Yakşagānamulu, Andhra University Series, No. 55, 1955).
44. Use of Āti and Rūpaka tāḷa are more in the compositions assignable to a later date.
45. Ardha Çaṅdrikā, Dhavala, Rāgada and other names disappear. They are superceded by Dāru.
46. Thanjai Mannar Serfōji SM Library. (Bundle D. 852. D. Catalogue. Telugu manuscripts D. 853) About two hundred eight Padās are preserved. Also, refer Chapters III & IV, Supra.
47. Even before his time the influence could be felt in rāgas like Jogi Asāveri, Bilāval, and Bṛṁdāvani handled by Giriṛāja Kavi. Śṛṁgāra padās of Giriṛāja Kavi in praise of Serfōji and spiritual compositions of Sadāśiva Brahmē ṅdra are valuable.
48. Ms. D. Nos. 446, 447 (T.M. S.S.M. Library) The manuscripts contain Padās in praise of patrons by court poets.
49. D. Nos. 633-34. T.S.S.M. Library Catalogue of Telugu Mss.
50. Bhōnsle Vaṁśa Çaritram. (T.M.S.S.M. Library Series, No. 46, 1951).
51. T.V. Kuppuswami and T.K. Venkatasubramanian : Rhythm in historical cognition (Kalinga Publications, Delhi, 1993).
52. Subbarāma Dikṣitar: Saṅgīta Sampradāya Pradarśini. (Music Academy, Madras). These volumes give biographical sketches of composers and random samples of their compositions.
53. A Nādasvara party with Tamil vidwāns was known as Periya meḷam.
54. They are the disciples of Muttuswāmī Dikṣitar who is said to have appreciated the compositions and conferred the title 'Bharata Śrēṣṭāḷ' on the quartette.
55. At present, performances begin invoking the blessings of Gaṇesh (Vināyaka). It is followed by Alārippu when the dancer appears on the stage.
56. Rhythmic syllable : 'Ta-Ti-Dhin-Datta' Singing of Tiruppukaḷ (Aruṇagirināthar—Supra) serves as background while Naṭṭuvanār spells rhythmic syllables. If Tiruppukaḷ is not included, the syllables are sung in Pañçama or top Ṣadja in the rāga Nāṭṭai.

57. Ṣolkaṭṭu—e.g.: 'Tadana, ṭandana tadimi dindimi'.

58. Vide supra Chapters II & III.

59. Anne Marie Gaston : Development of the repertoire in Modern Bharatanaṭyam. (The Journal of the Music Academy, Madras, Vol. LXII - 1991) pp. 95-134.

60. Anne Marie Gāston : Continuity and recreation in the performing arts of India; A study of two artistic traditions. (D. Phil. thesis. Oxford University).

61. Ashok D. Ranade : Devotional music in India (Saṅgīta Nāṭaka Academy, No. 85-86, July-December, 1987, p. 41.

62. At the Vijayanagara court there were several vocalists who specialised in Svara Pallavīs.

    Y. Satyanarayana Rao : Svara Pallavī and Jakkini Daruvulu (*The Journal of the Music Academy*, Vol. XXXVI, 1965, pp. 105-12.

63. Ref : Saṅgītakalānubhava.

64. Supra Chapters II-IV.

65. Vīrāḷimalai Kuṛavaṅçi with which the Dēvadāsis of the temple are associated had been collected and edited by N. Syāmaḷa. (Department of Music, Madras University, Madras, 5).

66. He also authored Bahattara meḷa rāgamālika in Marātti. (Seventy-two meḷa rāgamālika). Later Mahā Vaidyanāthier composed in Sanskrit. (Praṇatārtihara Prabhō Murārē) with the opening section in Śrī Rāga.

67. I had the privilege of meeting Nāgarāja Rāo, a surviving Lāvaṇi singer. He is also the author of Svāyi (a title given to the group which wins in a context).

68. Reasons for composing are stated :

    "Kāvaḍiççināvallūrōr Poovaṭiççindēvalutta
    -kkāḷaiyām Asan-aliççōrççintayē—enta
    veḷaiyum mahilnturappōr nintayē"

    Tunes are the same as those of Aṇṇāmalai Reddiar's. It indicates the popularity of Reddiar's compositions. So far we have twenty two compositions in print (Aṇṇāmalai Reddiar's). Editions however abound in mistakes. Śuddhānanta Bhārati's and K.V. Śrinivāsa Iyeṅgar's editions are also available. Kāvaṭi Cindu editions :

    Kaḷkuḷam Kuppuswami Mudaliyar (Madras, 1904)

    Padmanābha Vilāsa Printing Works (1907)

    V.V. Nārayaṇaswāmī Mudaliar. (1914)

    Yālpāṇam Paruttiturai Brahma-sri S. Subramaṇia Śāstirkal (1928)

    Śakti Kāryālaya. (1950). (This is a fairly good edition).

    With notation

    K.V. Śrīnivāsa Iyeṅgar: Saṅgīta ÇittiraikKōvai. (12 Nos.). (Poomakaḷ Company).

Peruṅkuḷam Śrīnivāsa Iyeṅgar: Saṅgīta Anubhavasāra Saṅgraham (Four Nos.).

B.R.V. Press, Triplicane, Madras (1986, Aṇṇāmalai Reddiyar in Kāvaṭic-ciṅdu, Many Nos.).

69. 'Pravēśika' of Nāṭyaśāstra. (Entry of a leading character on the stage) has a parallel in 'Patrapravēśa' Daru of Bhāgavata mēḷa and Kuṟavañci-nāṭakas.

70. Kaṇḍakūru Rudra Kavīs 'Sugrīva Vijayam' (u). The poet flourished in Kṛṣṇadeva Rāya's court. The work is full of complicated metrical verses.

71. Few examples are : Dharmapurī Subbarāyar (1900),

Tiruppaṇaṅdāl (Taḷavanam) Paṭṭābhirāmayya. (1863).

Paṭṭanam Subramania Iyer (1845-1902), Tiruppati Nārāyaṇaswāmī, (1873-1912).

72. Dṛśya Kāvyas like 'Pallakki Sēvā Prabandham', 'Viṣṇu Pallakki Śiva Prabandham', 'Saçi Purandaramu', 'Satidana Suramu'. These works bear Sahāji's ankitas (pen names) such as Tyāgēśa Bhūpa, Tyāga soura, Tyāgamurāri.

73. Sahaji: Kalinatana Samvādam (T.M.S.S.M. Library).

74. In Jakkiṇi Daru terms like 'Ellilam', 'Ellamale' are used frequently.

75. King Tulajāji's 'Śivakāmasuṅdarī Pariṇayanāṭakam' (T.M.S.S.M.L.) contains varṇana and samvāda Darūs.

76. Examples 'Paḷam naḷuvi pālil viḷundārpōlē'

'Pāmpiṟkku pāl vārka vārka'.

77. 'Negutādittidi' in Telugu.

78. Anulōma-Vilōma Daru is tuned, in Gaṅgātaraṅgiṇī rāga and rūpaka tāḷa. (Sārasa daḷa nayanā).

79. In 'Prahḷādaçaritra' each character introduces himself/herself through a Pravēśa Daru.

80. Mēruswāmī alias Ānanda Padmanābha Goswāmī is the earliest popular Kīrtankār known to us. Rāja Serfōji (1798 to 1882) and Śivāji II (1832 to 1855) were his patrons. He visited the court of Swāti Tirunāḷ of Travancore in A.D. 1836.

81. Kṛṣṇa Bhāgavatar of Tanjore did it.

82. Prameeḷa Gurumūrthy : Kathā Kālakṣēpa—a study. (International Society for Investigation of Ancient Civilisations, Madras, 32, 1994).

5
Hermeneutics

'TONAL MUSIC' attempts to make people believe in the consensual representation of the world. In Tamil Nadu the first stage of the attempt is marked by "sacrifice", characterised by ritual practices. Right from this stage, music is a professional activity. The Āḻvārs and Nāyanmārs made use of it as a medium to propagate their religious dogmas. With the advent of the Nāyak and Marāta rule at Thanjāvūr, music becomes a saleable asset. An endless period of 'Reproduction' follows, matching the creation of demand. Music compositions are canonised and catalogued. The trend continues till this day. In the process of transformation arises a symbolic confrontation between "Joyous enjoyment and austere power".[1] Signification of music becomes a "relation embedded in a specific culture." "Musical message" is expressed in a global fashion in its operationality. It is no longer a mere juxtaposition (signification) of each sound element.

In the course of their fluctuating history, the Tamils have not suffered a total overthrow. Most of the threads are intact. Sequence of development components run parallel to renovation of culture.[2] Music fulfils a precise function in social organisation. Music gains a meaning operationally beyond its own syntax, since music falls within the very power that produces society. Though "listening to music is to receive a message" it is difficult to equate music with a language.

Words of a language refer to "signified music". Music never refers to a code of linguistic type. "It is not a myth coded in sounds instead of words; but rather a language without meaning."[3] It has neither meaning nor finality and Claude—Levy Strauss attempts to fix music into the double structure of language by distinguishing within it a signifier and a signified. He superimposes a semantic system on sounds.

The other extreme view is that "there is no music before language". This is a theoretical hypothesis which suggests that the origin of music should not be sought in linguistic communication. It is known that the drum and song have long been carriers of "linguistic meaning". Yet there is no convincing theory of music as language. Evidently, signification of music is very complex.

It is not surprising that origin of music remains a speculation. Literary works in Tamil narrate that the Tamilians enjoyed music in the ripple of waters, the roar of thunder, waves of sea, splash of waterfalls, hum of the bells, the chuckle and chirps of birds. Numerous references in Tamil literature compare music to sounds of nature.[4] "Saṅgīta Makạrandam" authored by Nārada (?) designates nature-based music as "Anāgata Saṅgīta",[5] that is a "sound that directly emanates from the sky". These views defy rational analysis. Western scholars are of the view that music originated with the particular effort of man to evoke desired feelings in the listeners.[6] The Indian view is that the soul desiring to speak out its intention, ignites the mind. The mind operates in the vital heat of the body and sets the air in motion. The air thus stimulated produces sound.[7] Logically, any sound of definite pitch is a musical sound and such sounds pre-date human race.

Artistes and aestheticians of Indian music have realised the blending of "aesthetic emotional expressions, musical improvisations, rhythmic time-measures and spiritual experiences" as the soul of music and dance. Vocal music, instrumental music and dance in harmonious combination came to be known as "Saṅgīta". Among the demi-gods and goddesses, the Gandharvas are the supreme singers and the Apsarā maidens are unmatched dancers. The traditional sixty-four arts (Catuṣṣaṣṭīkalās) comprise of all the arts including fine-arts. The number sixty-four is illustrative but not exhaustive. With efflux of time, fresh contributions to fine-arts, industrial arts and new techniques of artistic expressions have been absorbed while some of the older forms and techniques have fallen into disuse—'Gandharva Veda' including Nātya Veda is one of the four Upa Vedas (subsidiaries).

Weber, the western musicologist suggests that "a society could be judged by its sounds, by its art than by its statistics".[8] Music is an instrument of understanding. It prompts us to decipher a "sound form". "It is a play of mirrors in which every activity is reflected, defined, recorded and distorted".[9] This complex mirror yields a vision that is rich. For Karl Marx "Music is the mirror of reality", for Nietzsche "Expression of truth"; for Freud "A text to decipher."

Ilaṅkō Aṭikal, author of the Tamil epic Śilappatikāram refers to various forms of collective singing.[10] This tradition of collective singing had influenced the Āḷvārs and Nāyaṅmārs. Tiruvāçakam authored by Saint Māṇickavāśakar contains Pāvai, Ammānai, Sunnam, Tumbi, Teḷḷenam, Salal, Pūvalli, Untiyar Tolnuṇukkam and Ulā. All these varieties are folk-formats, Nālāyira Prabhaṅdam contains Kummi, Paraṇi, Paḷḷu, Kuram, Kuravaṅçi Noṇḍināṭakam, Veṇṇilaikaṇṇi and Çiṅtu (variety of compositions).

In the Tamil tradition "Tevārappaṇ' is the earliest example of musical composition. It is made up of "Patikams". Each 'Patikam' has a collection of groups of ten or twelve verses. 'Patikam' is recited without break. Some scholars affirm that the music of the stanza of Patikam had inspired composers of Aṣṭapati (Jeyadēva). Prabhaṅda, Eka-dhātu kīrtana, etc.[11] Hymns contain 'Stala' or 'Vākgēyakāra' mudras.[12] Views about the structure of the Patikams differ. But music, word and thought content are all blended in a harmonious unit.

By a dexterous use of the Tamil language, embellishments, unique in character, are introduced.[13] "Koṇḍukkatti" enhances the beauty of the Tevāram 'Aḍuttānai'.[14] Hymns of Sambandar are rich in "Ēkapādam".[15] Alliteration (anuprāsa) is liberally used. The first hymn of Saṁbaṅdar (in the paṇ Naṭṭapālai) can be cited as an example.[16] The melodic structure is suitable for congregational rendering. At the same time, an individual too can render it competently. Supernatural gifts and patronage are claimed for those who render Patikams flawlessly. This is popularly known as "Palaśṛuti".[17]

To arrange each Patikam in a chronological sequence is difficult. It is however claimed that the sacred hymns of Āḷvārs and Nāyaṅmārs were arranged in canonical form in the eleventh century A.D.[18] Epigraphical evidences prove that number of shrines were constructed in honour of the "Samayāçāryas" (Āḷvārs and Nāyaṅmārs) during the interval ninth to thirteenth centuries A.D. In course of time, these memorials acquire the status of full-fledged temples. Monasteries (Maṭhās), have been built in commemoration of Tēvāram trio. Epigraphs of the thirteenth century refer to "Guhais". These are Maṭhās named after Tirugñānasambandar.[19] Palm-leaf manuscripts preserved by these Maṭhās contain hymns of the Tévāram trio.

Divyaprabaṅdhams of Vaiṣṇavite Āḷvārs are four thousand in number. In assigning chronological limits to these compositions, tradition and history do not always agree. Mudalāyiram, Periya Tirumoḷi, Iyarpā and Tiruvāimoḷi (four) have poetic merit, meant to be recited. The others (three) are known as 'Iśaipā', meant to be sung. Written records are not available and perhaps this had caused the tunes pass into oblivion.[20] The text forms part of the canonical literature used in temples. Each temple choir must have had its own method of (style) rendering. Though the original music element is lost the instinct for creative expression had been preserved.

Max Weber describes western music as one of the peculiar forced product derived from the rational enclave of monastic life in the middle ages. This "technical factor" of Weber includes script or notation.[21] In the fourteenth century church-music became secularised.[22] It became autonomous from the chant. The exact origin and early history of chants remain controversial topics. The first important effort is believed to be that of St. Ambrose, Bishop of Milan (A.D. 374 to 397). He recognised Latin as the language of liturgy. This was superseded by the "Gregōrian Chant" named after Pope Gregōry (A.D. 590 to 604).

The simplest form of psalm chant has an intonation (opening phrase); a 'Tuba'.[23] (reciting note) and a variety of phrases ending with "Amen". 'Amen' was sung at the end by the congregation. The modes are in sets of eight, each built around a certain pitch. Each has a dominating note...the reciting note fixed for psalms—the Tuba (Vādi: ?). The note on which the psalm ends is the commencing note of the mode (Nyāsa?). All the modes are semi-tones. Ambrōsian modes are called "authentic" and the Gregorian "phlagal". Each phlagal starts on a perfect fourth (Samvādi?) below the authentic. Gregorian chants have specific characteristics: (a) melodies are designed for individual singing, (b) rhythm of music is the rhythm of prose and not customary poetry, (c) purpose is not to delight the senses but to move the listener prompting worship, (d) 'scales' are modes not patterns. Absence of accompanying instruments is also to be noted.[24]

The Indian conception of a musician is that "he is a reporter and a prophet".[25] 'Pāṇan' of the Saṅgam-age of Tamil history is an outcast. He serves as a social historian. He highlights virtues and never hesitates to point out vice. By the seventh century A.D. the Pāṇan (wandering minstrel) becomes an ācārya.[26] He is adored. In the social hierarchy, his status gets elevated. One of the important duties of the Pāṇan of the Saṅgam-age is to wake up the king early in the morning. The later acāryas woke up the presiding deity in temples.

It is indeed interesting to note that in all ancient civilisations, the musician had been a slave or untouchable person. Even as late as the twentieth century, Islam prohibits believers from eating at the same table with a musician. In Persia, music was for a long time an activity identified with prostitutes. History tells us that ancient religions admitted a caste of priests to perform service to the lord of the temple. Mythology endows such priest-musicians with super-natural and civilising powers. Orpheus domesticated animals and transplanted trees. Amphion attracted fish and Anion built the walls of Thebes.[27] Musicians earned popularity by curing diseases (therapeautic) Pythagorus and Emphydocles cured the possessed; and Ismenius cured sciatica, David cured Saul's madness by playing his harp.

In wealthy monarchies of the west, the 'orchestra' had always been a display of power. The music code of China has five words: Palace, Deliberation, Horn, Manifestation and Wings.[28] The number and arrangement of the musicians indicated the status of the lord who patronised the orchestra. (A 'Square' for the emperor and "Three rows" for the dignitaries). The emperor authorised the form of music that would assure good order within society and prohibited those that might trouble the people.

Throughout the ancient world what we notice is the "concern for controlling music".[29] The Dionecian rites in Greece, Rome and other cults originating in Asia minor are examples of "Popular music". They had always managed to survive. At odds with official religions and centres of power, these rites gathered marginals and society tolerated them. In Rome, however, we hear of efforts to suppress such growth. Charlemagne (emperor) forced cultural unity by enforcing the practice of "Gregōrian chant", resorting to armed force to accomplish that end. In Milān, which remained faithful to Ambrōsian liturgy, hymnals were burnt in the public square.

The Jongleur (traditional musician) is the leading figure in the Middle-Ages. He remained outside society.[30] The Church condemned him accusing him of paganism and magical practices. The Jongleur had no fixed employment. He moved from place to place offering his services in private residences. He created music and carried it with him and completely organised its circulation within the society. Some of the Jongleurs played from memory. If a melody was popular, numerous texts appeared based on it. The styles functioned essentially within the same structures and were used interchangeably. They used their talents to sing the praise of the patrons. The circulation of the music was neither elitist nor monopolistic of creativity. The European "feudal world" with its polyphony remained a "world of circulation" in which music in daily life was inseparable from lived time in which it was active, not something to be watched.

In secularised church-music (14th century A.D.) Higni Angles finds Indian influence.[31] Gregorian chants are modal which are sung and not recited. Comparing them with the hymns (compositions of Āḻvārs and Nāyaṅmārs) is admissible. Yet, the comparison could not be carried too far. The chants are recited adhering to protocols and time schedules.[32] Pronunciation of the text is emphasised. For instance till the 4th century A.D., the Greek language was used in Roman churches too. Latin replaced Greek only in sixth century A.D. The common factor (east or west) in the equation, is Bhakti.

Between the fourteenth and sixteenth centuries, salaried musicians become popular in Europe. Musician got the appellation "Minstrel" (Menestral or Menestriar derived from Latin 'Ministerialis' meaning functionary). Musician was no longer a 'nomad' but a settled citizen of a town. The minstrels organised themselves into guilds after those of the craftsmen and merchants. They had a patron saint as their leader (St. Julian of the minstrels). They had their annual meetings. Municipal legislation ensured their welfare by granting them disability dues and retirement benefits. Musicians acquired a new social position. A captivating account of this transformation is given by Johann Joachim Quantaz (A.D. 1697 to 1773). He was a Jongleur to begin with became a minstrel and finally was a flute master to the Russian King, Frederick II.[33]

In Europe, 'music' was a 'power'—ritual power, representative power and bureaucratic power too. Basically, music is claimed to be intuition—a path to knowledge. The Greek philosopher Aristotle enumerates three kinds of music (a) Ethical (useful for education), (b) Of action (those which influence audience who do not know to perform), and (c) Cathartic (aim to perturb and appease).[34] Spengler distinguishes between "Appolonian music" (modal, monodic with an oral tradition) and "Faustian music" (tonal, polyphonic with a written tradition). These are non-functional categories. Every code of music is rooted in the ideologies and technologies of its age.

In Peninsular India, it is Rāmamātya who heralds a new era. Rāmamātya, author of Svaramelakaiānidhi declared "Music has its theory and it has to abide by it...but in the case where theory appears to be violated more often, it is found that the sweetness suffers nothing thereby. In practical music, the basis is more important than its theory. Give it up for the sake of theory, then you use the pleasant effect due to the art-side. There it is! Sweet music has lived in this world as an art.[35] Since the days of Rāmamātya 'Vīṇā (musical instrument) serves as an indicator or pathfinder.[36] During the time of Śārṅgadēva (12th century A.D.) seven Vikṛta svaras had to be accommodated in a 'Vīṇā' with five frets.[37] Rāmamātya resorted to a technical strategy. Goviṅda Dīkṣitar and Veṅkaṭamakin who appear later are indebted to Rāmamātya for the knowledge of the 'Vīṇā' with four strings intended to be played, three drone and tāḷa strings and fixed frets. Rāmamātya's treatment of the Suddaméḷa, Madyaméḷa and Regunātamēḷa had encouraged the introduction of Vīṇā with twelve frets by Goviṅda Dīkṣitar.[38] Veṅkaṭamakin effected further improvements by systematising tuning and fretting. The Vīṇā with twenty-four frets marks the final stage of such progress.[39]

Rāmamātya was able to accommodate the seven Vikṛta-svaras in five frets by resorting to the following strategy:

1. Çyuta Saḍja	1. Çyuta Niṣāda
2. Sādhāraṇa Gāṅdhāra	2. Same

3. Aṅdara Gāṅdhāra	3. Cyuta madhyama gāndhāra
4. Cyuta madhyama	4. ————
5. Cyuta Paṅcama	5. Cyuta Paṅcama (ma)
6. Kaisiki nisāda	6. Same
7. Kākali niṣada	7. Same.

Medieval authors who take the cue from Rāmamātya are classified as "southern". The result is the reconciliation of svara names of Śārṅgadeva (valid for the Grāmamūrçana system) with the system of twelve fixed notes in an octave. On account of the fixation of 'Sa' and 'Pa' as immovable points in the octave during the medieval period, the 'mēḷa system' comes into existence. The difference of "Pramāna Śruti" between Paṅcama of Ṣadjagrāma and Madhyamagrāma loses significance. 'Sa' becomes the fixed tonic of all ragas. The wide range of divergence in regard to ragas in all the works of the medieval period can never be missed. This change is yet to be explicitly acknowledged and lakṣaṇa granthakāras (authors of treatises) seem to have ignored it. The medieval period marks the crumbling down of some features of the ancient musical system. 'Vīnā' had played a considerable role in effecting this transformation.

The Nāyak and Marātta rulers of Tanjavūr extended patronage to music and dance. Since A.D. 1565 (Battle of Talaikkōṭṭa) small independent states sprang up in the south. "By the middle of the seventeenth century the musical centre of gravity shifted to Tanjore and the cream of Carnātic music was being churned out at this crucible of culture, which had been exposed to the influence of the north and to some extent of the west under the fostering care of the Nāyak and Maṛaṭṭa rulers".[40] T. Veṅkataswāmī Rao, author of the 'District Manual of Tanjore' (Part II) observes "Of the native musical art, Tanjore perhaps has been the only seat, properly so called, south of the Kṛṣṇa since the fall of the Hindu Empire of Vijayanagar."[41] Tanjore had also been the seat of Vijayālaya Cōla rulers.

"The period of the Nāyak Kings of Tanjore was in splendour and richness of output, the immediate corollary of the period of Kṛṣṇadeva Rāya of Vijayanagar."[42] Nāyak patronage cculd be epitomised. It manifested itself in the shape of (a) appointment of professional composers, performers to serve in the court,

(b) construction of auditoriums, (c) concerts in the royal durbar, (d) liberal grants of land to musicians and artistes, (e) extension of facilities for cultural exchange, (f) encouragement of research in theory and practice of music, (g) encouragement of manufacture of musical instruments, (h) appointment of supervisors to supervise the execution of schemes, (i) endowment to temples for purposes of maintaining artistes and (j) establishment of a College of Oriental learning with music as a core subject.

The seventeenth, eighteenth and nineteenth centuries witness unprecedented progress in theory and practice of Carnātic music. The roots of the arts of dance and music which are current could be traced back to this epoch. By the time of the rule of the Tanjore Nāyaks, lakṣaṇagranthas (musical treatises) have been accepted. They lent support for consolidation of "Art music". The Vīṇā with twenty-four frets had ushered in the 'Tanjore mēḷam'. Veṅkaṭamakin systematised the seventy-two mēḷakartas and laid the foundation of the edifice. Lakṣaṇa and Lakṣya (theory and practice) were happily blended and the best music talents flocked to Tanjore. A careful scrutiny of the lakṣya aspect (theory) shows both obsolete sançāras (non-current contours) and sançāras in vogue (contours current) in respect of rāga-ālāpana (delineation). 'Melodic individualities' of many rāgas come to be well-defined only after the eighteenth century.[43] Musical formats like Kṛti, Kirtana, Varṇa, Rāgamālika, etc. are not cited as lakṣyas. They must have gained currency, but not classification. Rāgas have come to be a group under seventy-two mēḷakartas.

Such developments could not have been effected in a vacum. The progress recorded at Tānjāvūr (seventeenth to the nineteenth centuries) shows that the "concern of tradition is the present and the future." Those who felt guided and sheltered by standard institutions and habitual patterns of perceptions from previous centuries seem to have felt confident and foreseen a future which did not radically differ from the present.[44] Idea of progress is in-built in all these endeavours. Theory of music had been stripped of its mythical aura under rigorous practical application (Lakṣya). Mute submission to the authority of the past was replaced by other patterns of behaviour such as "impulse to rejuvenate". This certainly is an attempt to renew contact with tradition. The works of the period appear to be parts of a living tradition and determinants of the future. Rāmamātya's break (from Śārṅgadēva) with tradition is not revolutionary. It was not also without jolts since the 'core factors' asserted their influence in the process.

It should however be realised that what was achieved is not a mere repetition of technical exercises. The reconstructed scheme took on the appearance of a musical reminiscence of the long-last past. A vein of nostalgia is unmistakable. Modes did change character when they were transplanted. Aesthetics turn towards "programme music", modifications are brought in and the innovations serve the largest interest of preservation. By the last quarter of the eighteenth century the key structure had become very much refined. Thematic and motivated developments characterise the entire change.

In aesthetic perception "conservatism" (in maintaining tradition) gives place to novel interpretation of musical works. This justifies the view that "music is historic through and through". That means that core characters are inviolable. "Historical analysis" and "aesthetic experience" are not two compartments of art. The historians believe that the past and present form an indissoluble alloy. The remote is perceived as such and yet experienced as near and the ultimate result is a "twisted aesthetic paradox". What we perceive is the emancipation of the art towards "aesthetic autonomy". In the evolutionary history of music, lakṣaṇa (theory) always follows lakṣya (practice). Musical practice undergoes changes from time to time and lakṣaṇa tries to interpret lakṣya current in the different epochs. Thus the evolution of theory and prevalence of different views with reference to practice unambiguously reflect the progressive nature of the art.

The European experience (described earlier) brings out the importance of the expression of "consciousness of an epoch". Musical impact of the West on our music is practically non-existent. In the use of instruments, the violin had become an inseparable companion. The clarionet, is another. Other instruments have been admitted into the mainstream of our instrument varieties.[45] The system of European notation had been adopted. Clues denoting duration of half, quarter and one-eighth units are utilised.[46]

There had been an indigenous system of notation based on

solfa letters. "Likhitapātha" (written lessons) was not felt necessary when the Gurukula system was popular. When music came to be taught to large groups in institutions, the need for a system of notation arose. Many codes were designed by native musicologists to denote the octave, duration, grace, pitch, variety of a note and the time signatures. Introduction of printing made the use of certain signs possible, which could not have been used while recording on palm-leaves. 'Notation' is an attempt to preserve what should primarily be heard and this is true of all music. Notated music by a Spanish composer for instance, means little to a Scottish player. Problems of Gamakas and other nuances had not arisen in Western music. Notation is useful to the individual familiar with the system concerned.

Advent of 'art-musical concerts' widened the scope of rhythmic accompaniments. Instrumental music is independent of language (text). Rāga and rāga delineation received particular attention at the hands of the instrumentalists. In this context, Nādasvaram players' contribution is praiseworthy. Utility of Mṛdanga as an ideal rhythmic accompaniment in concerts is being increasingly recognised. In the "Tanjore style of percussion accompaniment" great emphasis is laid on "quality to please" (Śrāvya).[47]

It should be recalled that "Meḷaprastāra" is an important contribution to musicology. Yet, its practical value is a much debated theme. Formulation of twenty-two or twenty-four svarastānas is of academic interest. Those based on twelve svarastānas has practical as well as theoretical values. Çaturdaṇḍi compositions cover a range of more than two octaves. Lakṣaṇa graṅtas, Prabhaṅdas and Thāyas of the period have number of prayōgas in "Maṅdra" and "Tāra" octaves. Kṛtis and Rāgamālikas (deemed as chronologically later) are mostly in the Madhyasthāyī with frequent flights into Tārasthāyī paṅçama (pa) and Madhyama (ma). Çaturdaṇḍi exhibits a preference to Maṅdra sthāyī. This is significant, as it suggests that Tārasthāyī exposition must have been popular. Maṅdra prayōgas must have been sung in Maṅdra sthāyī.[48]

It is claimed that "Harikatha Kālakṣepam" as an artform entered Tamil Nadu during this epoch, due to Marātta influence.[49] Metrical forms like Śāki, Diṇḍi, Ōvi, Paṅçapati were adopted. Dēśāti, Madhyāti tāḷas, Yēḷati tāḷas and rāgas like Behāg, Pīlu, Kāpi, Tilang were incorporated.

The main subject matter of music-history is always the "primary substance of music". With every new epoch, the emphasis shifts. Past views are not suppressed by successors. The initiative for innovation patently operated during the Nāyak-Marātta rule of Tanjore. The 'element of function' had not been irrelevant. Functional notion dominates the court-music of Tanjāvūr. But the representational aesthetic drawing from ancient theories had not been a casualty. A healthy relation grew between the end that music was intended to serve and the technical means considered to be appropriate to achieve that end. There had been no confrontation between ends and means. The "autobiography in notes" that characterises the age, has a latent meaning that could find expression only through spiritual identification. A cross-section of the present day music-lovers claim that the Nāyak-Marātta period is a replacement of the 'personal view of music' by a 'structural' one. Even those who understand little about 'structural analysis' respect its authority. Whatever may be the view, our greater concern is with the "evolved product" which commands respect at home and abroad.

REFERENCES

1. T.V. Kuppuswami : Musical Historicism—A Case Study (Trends in Social Research, Delhi 92, Vol.I, No. 2, December 1992) pp. 75-78.
2. T.V. Kuppuswami : Carnātic music and the Tamils *op. cit.*

   T.V. Kuppuswami and T.K. Venkatasubramanian : Rhythm in Historical Cognition (Kalinga Publication, Delhi).
3. Claude Levi Strauss : The Naked Man (Tr)

   John and Dorean Weightman (London, Jonathan Cape, 1981) pp. 467, 659.
4. Paripāṭal, Kuruṅtokai, Akanānūṛu, etc.
5. The work is dated Seventh Century A.D.

   "Ākāśa sambāvoradōya so anāhata Saṅgīta"
6. The Holy Bible declares "In the beginning was the word and the word was with God" (St. John : I)

   "Extremes of joy and sorrow warrant singing", (Taylor : Anthropology).
7. Tolkāppiyam refers to modes of production of sound and varieties of sound (Ōśai)

   Pirappial : 3,5,6,15,16

   Nūṅmarapu : 3: 33

8. Max Weber: Value Judgement in Social Science. Selections in translation (ed) W.G. Runciman (Cambridge University Press, 1978), p. 95.
9. *Ibid.*
10. Aōiççiyar Kuravai, Kuṅṛakkuravai, Vēṭṭuvari, Kaṇḍukavari, Ammānai Vari, etc.
11. There is no "Pallavi" for the singer to repeat. In a Tēvāram, this sometimes figures at the tail-end.
12. "Mudra" is in Tirukkataikkāppu in the Patikams of Gñānasambaṅdar and Sundarar.
13. The hymn of Tirugnañāsambaṅdar in the paṇ 'Kauśikam' can be cited as an example. The technique is "Mālaimāṟṟu" (Savya-Apasavya).
14. Metrical structure of a line gradually extends in perfect alignment with the meaning intended to be conveyed. Sanskrit literary convention calls it "Śrōtovaha Yati" (Uṟṟumai sērvatu Meyyinayē - in paṇ paṅçuram).
15. A particular line is repeated in subsequent stanzas (The word contents: e.g. Piramapiraturai pemmān yemmān-paṇ Vyāḷakkuriṅçi).
16. Tōduṭaya Śeviyiṇ Vitai ēriya tūvan matisūdi".
17. Çaritra Kīrtanas, Yakṣagānas, dramas and Kathākālakṣēpams normally conclude with the enumeration of Palaśṛti, e.g. Patikam on the presiding deity at Śirkāḷi temple in paṇ Vyalakkuṛiṅçi-Gñānasambaṅdar Gñānattamiḻnaṇkuara.
18. K.A. Nilakaṇṭa Śāstri : The Çōḷas, *op. cit.*, p. 637.
19. Many such Mathas (Guhais) could be found in the Tanjāvūr district. Annual reports on Epigraphy 233 of 1917,156 of 1911, 199 of 1932-33.......etc.

    T.V. Kuppuswami : Carnātic music and the Tamils, *op. cit.*, Chapter IV.
20. In this respect they are comparable with the Early Church-music of Europe.
21. Max Weber: Value Judgement in Social Science, *op. cit.*, pp. 98-100.
22. *Ibid.*
23. 'Tuba' is a trumpet, having only one note.
24. 'Organ' was included later, during the Middle Ages.
25. Supernatural powers have been attributed to them.
26. We hear of Tirunīlakaṇṭa Yālpāṇar. The general appellation however yields to the new designation Nāyanmār. Functions performed are mostly the same.
27. Many such miracles are said to have been performed by Nāyaṅmārs and Āḻvārs and other celebrities of later epochs.
28. Marina Sona bines : Le language musical (T) (Paris, Minuit, 1963).
29. Montesquieu (French) seems to have understood this phenomenon.

Montesquieu: The Spirit of the Laws. (Tr)
Thomas Nugent (New York, Hafner Publishing Company, 1965)
He declares "For Greeks, music was a necessary pleasure—necessary for social passification, and a mode of exchange—the only one compatible with good morals."

30. 'Jongleur'—derived from the Latin word 'Joculare' (to entertain); designated vocalists and instrumentalists, mimes, acrobats, buffoons, etc.
31. The New Oxford Dictionary of Music', Prof. Welsch also refers to "Eastern influence" (Eastern elements in Western chants, Chapter on Early Medieval Music)
S.A.K. Doorga Tévāram and Gregōrian Chants
(Paṇ Ārōiçi Conference-Tamil Iśai Saṅgam 1986), pp. 94–103.
32. Edward Dickson : Music in the History of Western Church (1928). (Intruit, Communion, Iradual, Allelue are Church routine).
33. Jacques-Gabriel Frod : Home (ed) Ecritis des musicians (Paris Mercure de France, 1912), pp. 351-363.
34. Aristotle: Politics (Tr) (13399-13426).
35. "Tatra lakṣaṇnaodēna gāndhāram sāmprayujyatē"-
———————— Tasmāt lakṣyapradhānam gñānam lōkē pravar-tatē ,————————.
(Svaramēḷa Kalānidhi A.D. 1550).
36. Antique "Yāḻ" of Tamil tradition is superceded. "Māśil Veeṇaiyum", the hymn is often quoted in support of their claim.
37. Out of twelve frets in an octave, seven had to be allocated for Śudda svaras.
38. The treatise "Saṅgīta Sūḍa" furnishes details in this regard.
39. S.Ramanathan : Reghunātha meḷa Vīṇā.
(Journal of the Music Academy, Madras, 1964), pp. 143-47.
A.V. Kamala: The evolution of the Viṇā (Unpublished thesis, University of Madras, Madras-5)
Smt. Vidyasankar: The Process of Viṇā fretting
(Journal of the Music Academy, 1959), p. 129.
40. S. Seetha : Tanjore as a seat of music during the seventeenth, eighteenth and nineteenth centuries (University of Madras, 1981), pp. 7-8.
41. T. Venkasami Rao: Manual of the Tanjore District, Part II, p. 287.
42. P.P.S.Sastry : The Decennial Catalogue of Telugu manuscripts, Introduction III.
43. S. Seetha : Tanjore as a seat—*op. cit.* furnishes details (Lakṣaṇa).
44. Determining a rāga by quoting Geeta, Ālāpa, Udgraha, Rūpaka, Thāya. Daru and Prabhaṅda prayōga is first seen in Maharāja Sahāji's Rāgalakṣaṇa, work.

Vide Supra : Chapter II.

45. Muttuswāmī Dīkṣitar had adopted the melody "God save the King" (the then National Anthem). He has introduced certain innovative changes. The rāga "Katanakutūhalam" assigned to Paṭṇam Subramania Iyer, shows Western influence.

46. Rev M.A. Popely makes an appeal for an All India System of Notation (Ref : Journal of Music Academy, Madras, 1930)

    Pt. Subramaṇya Śāstri : A plea for a rational system of simplified notation (Journal of Music Academy, Madras, 1931)

    S. Vidya: Gamaka signs in music notation (Journal of Music Academy, 1943).

47. Nārāyaṇaswāmī Appa, Vaidyanātha Iyer, Tukāram and Dāsswāmīkaḷ set the trend.

48. Ālāpa and Thāya belong to the branch of Manodharmasaṅgīta. Compositions were illustrations. "Music for practice" (Abyāsa) and 'model compositions' were well defined. We hear of specialists like Śaṅkarābharaṇa-Naraśa Iyer and Tōḍi Seetārāma Iyer. Compositions like "Gātra Daṇḍi" and "Jāntra Daṇḍi" were intended for learners. The former was for vocal practice and the latter for instrumental practice. These compositions cover a range of two or three stāyis.

49. Prameela Gurumūrthy: Kathākālakṣēpa—A study (International Society for the Investigation of Ancient Civilisations, Madras-32, 1994).

6
Epilogue

Since the time of the Greek philosopher Plato it is believed that artistic creation is not only a reflection of the present but also a memory of the past. Traditional art of music illustrates this forboding of Plato. Tradition links the artiste, the listener and the entire nation. It commands one to reflect on the emotional experience of the past. Respect and love for the past form the chief characteristics of Indian culture. Assimilation of cultural heritage is therefore considered a great asset. Artistic and cultural values cannot be divorced from the memory of the art of the past. The current of time does not go back but time is experienced in the consciousness of an artiste. He turns to the past to understand the present and anticipate the future. Art of the past is intensely assimilated, experienced and interpreted.

William Weber, an American musicologist points out to the special situation that developed in West European musical theory in the seventeenth and eighteenth centuries. He stresses that the most significant fact pertaining to the history of musical taste was that music "did not have a corpus of ancient works." Reconstruction of classical musical monuments failed. The speculation on ancient treatises took the place of an actual classical tradition. There were no concepts that would be sanctified by the creativity of classical authors. In musical practice there was no retrospective musical canonisation. A paradoxical situation thus arose. Musicologists turned to the aesthetic concepts of ancient treatises which had no direct bearing on the living musical practice of that epoch. A 'contamination' resulted. A speculative stratum, the stratum of 'philosophical interpretation' was projected. It stood in complex relations with the empirical basis of musicology. It became established in musical theory.

The study of the evolution of Carnātic music unfolds how the art had ever been dynamic, ever growing in form and expression, assimilating all that appealed. The savants who lived in the different epochs marking the stages of the development of the art harnessed inherited technical, ideological and social forces. In the light of their own experiences they related them to the future aims rationally. Critical understanding of the concepts and the conformity with the development of musical practice are witnessed throughout. Art is subjected to the changes in style and expression.

Religion had been an inseparable element of social life. Religion, philosophy and the art of music have been harmoniously blended in the Indian conception of 'God' (Supreme power) as *Nādabrahmam.* Music sprouts from the seeds of philosophy. With this background in spirituality, Indian music is supersensuous. The spring of Bhakti (devotion to a personal deity) inspired the finest art and literature. South India is a land of temples and these temples have been centres of music and dance. Music had been and is considered as the best offering to God. Music had become such a sublime fine-art that a dichotomy appears between music as 'a means of entertainment' and music 'as a means of self-realisation'.

Because of this background the professional musician of modern times faces a dilemma. If he wants to be popular, he has to mould his art to suit the demands of the average listener. The listener may not be artistically sensitive. The musician perhaps feels like lowering the standard. If the musician maintains the purity and sublimity of the art, he may not be popular. Music is the artiste's livelihood and the situation is a real challenging one. Mostly he performs to a 'mixed audience' that is 'sensible and insensible'. During the 'Great Age', some of the princes themselves were good musicians. The need for lowering the standard of the art perhaps never arose. Yet, in the atmosphere of the court, music seems to have lost much of its spiritual value. There had been the motivation to cater to sensual pleasure and music had become an instrument of providing entertainment. Compositions appeared praising the patron. This situation certainly must have increased the responsibility of the court-musician doubly. They had to cultivate 'good taste' or an appreciative audience who can listen to classical music. An overemphasis on the technical aspects of the art to the extent of drowning the aesthetic aspect could not be used either.

As for the 'Sāhitya' (text) literary content is secondary to melodious music as music tries to express through the medium of svaras. If literary expression and suitable note-patterns are blended harmoniously, emotional appeal is bound to increase. In absolute form, music had proved that it has inbuilt potential to express itself without the aid of literary content. A suitable text-pattern at the same time was necessary for attracting the lay-listener. Absolute form of music without words is expressed in 'instrumental music'. Vocal music uses note-patterns and words in such a way that their harmonious blend produces the desired effect. The demand could only be satisfied by creating 'taste for good music' in the listeners.

We often see that even an appreciative and critical listener returns from a concert hall overcome by a feeling of disappointment and pessimism. He cannot help recalling to himself the artistic heights touched by masters in the past whose haunting melodies and cadences linger in his memory. He compares the aesthetic delight of the music he had just heard with the ecstasy which he once experienced since listening to maestros of yesteryears. A young listener (one who had not the privilege of listening to maestros of yesteryears) is also capable of discerning whether the performer had accepted the norms in performing a composition or delineated a rāga satisfactorily.

What appears to be of supreme importance is whether the performer has succeeded in making music a vehicle of emotional appeal? The summum bonum of classical music is the experience of aesthetic delight. What seems to be necessary is a combination of 'tradition' with imagination, technique and grace. Classical music had been much propagated during the past half a century. At the same time problems have arisen in performing, listening and teaching. 'Concert music' (origins of which is traced to the Nāyak-Marātta rule) seems to be engaging the attention of music lovers, critics and other elite. Major points often made out are: (1) acrobatics dominate aesthetics ; (2) quality of patronage has deteriorated attitudes of listeners are casual, supercilious and condescending ; (3) predisposition towards names deflects the mind from appreciation and enjoyment ; (4) unqualified critics do more harm than good ; and (5) most of the defects of our current music spring from inadequate training.

'Acrobatics' in svara singing arises from an 'escapist mind' which cannot cope up with the aesthetic demand. This is basically a problem of the inferior or middling talent trying to walk into the shoes of the superior talent required to do justice to the on-the-spot creative music that Indian concert music demands. This again can be traced to the naive assumption that mere training and technique can make an artiste. This had virtually ended in concert platforms filled with aspirants good and bad. Training and performing constitute a cycle which can be vicious or virtuous.

In music we can roughly distinguish between two kinds of features. They may be called 'primary or direct appeals' and the 'indirect or secondary appeals'. Direct appeals are those characteristics which are more easily accessible like simple melodious lines and rhythms. Secondary appeals are more complicated embellishments and rhythmic variations which can be recognised by studying theories or long term exposure. Included in the latter are structural patterns of whole compositions and cycle structure of tāḷas. There are varieties of gradual transitions between primary and secondary appeals.

It is regrettable that scientific attitude had been absent from our musicology for quite a few centuries. The scientific or enquiring mind is aware that today is the fruit of yesterday. Such a mind is intuitive, free to enquire and examine its own intuition. Creative artistes belong to this category. For them history is in the nature of background material. Bharata, Śārṅgadeva, Ahōbala and others are 'men of science'. They have examined, logically defined musical processes and did not repeat historical texts. There are many areas of enquiry concerning 'technique'. For instance the question of 'Śruti' has always engendered more discussion than understanding. This problem had received an extraordinarily intuitive and intelligent consideration at the hands of ancients ; yet the vital clue is elusive. It is necessary to rethink about the nature of musical scales applying ideas and techniques of the 'mathematics of continuity and discontinuity'.

It is obvious that 'music is a message', but what exactly is the nature of the message? Can a musical meaning be understood by extra-musical medium? There have been vague talks about emotion, rasa, and music consisting mainly quotations from ancient texts. The hitherto untackled angle namely 'psychological' may bring out more clearly the 'meaning of music'. Music is a message (code). Its nature is stimulus and response. Its structure is to be carefully analysed and a reclassification of rāgas may be attempted. Aesthetic experience is to be inferred from the nature of its manifestations and the means for its achievement. Implementation is a characteristic of individual consciousness and culture. Personal illumination had been sought most frequently through the exercise of devotion, religious fervour and obedience. Anthropomorphic art had played a large part. Adoration and conviction had generated thought-forms. The number had increased. This never-ending chain of cause and effect heightens the aesthetic effects of these art-works. They became not only master-works of genius but powerful centres of the very aspirations they were meant to portray.

Boundaries of beauty (one aspect of reality) defy definition. Those who define art as that 'which is beautiful' have trapped themselves in their own limitations. Beauty as conceived by a person is highly individualistic. It is bound to change with personal consciousness and public opinion. Evidently 'impressionism' and 'spiritualism' heralded things and have served as direct forerunners of current interests. Music is a non-verbal act. Words spoken and written are the peculiar province of the mind. "They are the special tools of the fifth race—the people of the intellect." The artistes rationalise, differentiate and individualise. In non-verbal arts, the tendency is towards abstract symbolism. An important symptom of this consciousness is the increasing prevalance of creativity. Other things follow—wine is tasted while the wine is prepared by the individual himself. This freedom of ideation, whether partaking of another's art or creating one's own is the special forerunner of intuition for creativity. True creativity that touches the highest aspiration is the hallmark of the intuition.

The mathematics of continuity and discontinuity is another interesting field for investigation.[1] The fundamental problems of 'continuity-discontinuity' in all human perception is at the very foundation of the theory of 'Śṛutis'. The ancients have declared that at higher levels the 'Śṛutis' are indefinite. The notion of continuum is involved here. The reduction of the infinite to the cognisable and there from measurable finite, introduces approximations and errors. Śṛuti is the primordial prospective gap between time and non-time. For the purpose of final arithmetisation, the significant number twenty-two is attached to it. The concept of Śṛuti is to be used (as our ancients perceived it) as a pointer and not as a measure.

The very foundation of our Rāga system is the concept of Śṛuti. The Śṛutis are convenient steps of measurement of pitch analogous to 'Notes'. Pitch variations like the 'Vibrato' and the 'Thrills' are just below the conscience and perceivable only if attended to with a good deal of concentrated effort and that too in some cases only. There are many finer variations in pitch and duration which are completely missed by the conscience. In Indian music 'Gamakas' bear the burden of the unconscious forces and the 'Vibrato' is ruled out as unpleasant.[2] In the measurement of musical intervals and continuous transitions from note to note (Meeṇḍ, Jāru) we meet with the ultimate problem of the quantification of time. In the transition from note to note we come across with this problem. Of course we could bypass it through empirical and casual explanations meeting immediate emergencies.[3]

'Unison' or 'harmony' in music relates to pitch and tones. Saṅgita is the harmony between song and instruments, melody and time.[4] 'Laya' is defined (rhythm) as the 'unison of the phrases of the song' and 'phrases on the instruments' from the viewpoint of articulation and time.[5] Harmony relating to pitch and tones is technically called 'Śruti-laya' and the harmony relating to time is 'Tāḷa-laya'. Of Indian music it is said 'Śṛuti' is the mother and 'Laya' the father. Here 'Śṛuti' refers to the microtonic intervals making up an octave. It is those Śṛutis that play the notes of our music. Laya (rhythm) ensures discipline of the freedom of musical expression. Hence Tāḷa aspect of music is as important as the Rāga aspect. Tāḷa is almost indispensable in programmed music. In 'absolute music' (Ālāpana or delineation for instance) its role is minimal. In 'absolute music' it is more abstract and aims to produce formal beauty with minimum constraints possible. Laya's primary concern is the time-field and from this angle is spoken of as distinct from tāḷa.[6] Laya is defined as the time that is latent and pervasive amidst the beats as 'time-units in the admitted time-field'.[7] Time moves on unseen, effectively forgetting succession of forms and names. 'Kāla' is so called since it counts up details. Beats are counted up and drawn in a successive flow in the time-field. All of them are 'fleeting impressions.'

'Laya' is experienced through the web of tāḷas. It generates nascent emotion. The nature of emotional and mental impact that Laya has on the listener gives rise to the three-fold typology 'Madhya' (moderate); 'Viḷampita' (slackened) and 'Druta' (quickened). 'Madhya' provides to the listener a feeling of uniformity and continuity, 'Viḷampita' a feeling of leisurely movement and 'Druta' creates an illusion of speeding. Viḷampita is hard to be appreciated by a listener who lacks 'musical culture' since the auditory impressions are not apprehended as continuous or sequential. But a listener with a cultured musical ear will not fail to perceive the grandeur austere dignity and solace that the slow tempo evokes. The quick tempo evokes a sense of excitement and hence appeals easily. The moderate tempo appeals to the initiated and the non-initiated since auditory impressions are more or less uniform. It must be remembered that the effect is likely to wear off since the mind has a tendency to wander.

It is not necessary to take it for granted that all listeners would react to the tempos in an identical fashion. Individual response depends on temperament, prior association, priming, prevailing mood, knowledge of the composition and the like. These influencing factors may be termed as 'extra-musical'. What is to be understood is that rhythm facilitates the expression of emotions. The tempo might suggest and symbolise a mood, a feeling, an emotion or a disposition depending on the rhythmic patterns. The listeners' readiness to respond is an important condition.

An aspect of Laya which is rarely recognised is 'Tāḷa-bhāva'. We speak of 'Rāga-bhāva' meaning thereby that which constitutes the essential aesthetic uniqueness of a rāga. A tāla also has its own characteristic aesthetic value. Varieties of tālas have varying aesthetic effects. A medium tempo structure exhibited in a slow tempo can produce remarkably different aesthetic reaction. In Hindustānī music the exponents realise this potential even in rāga delineations. A particular set of svara phrases which project the bhāva of a rāga reveals the bhāva of another rāga, if handled in a slow tempo. It is well known that elongation or contraction of a 'note' in a rāga may change its bhāva altogether. This is suggestive of the fact that time-element has pronounced effect on the bhāva of a musical phrase. This is fully exploited in the art of dance. This goes by the name 'Kālapramāṇa' which means the tempo suitable to the purpose in view. The balancing of the sāhitya (text), the rāga, the tāḷa and the Kālapramāna are of vital importance.

Kālapramāṇa to some extent depends on the quality of the voice and the nature of the instrument used. Vīṇā for instance demands slackening of the tempo and flute music quickening of the tempo for producing the desirable effect. To play a composition (accepted by concensus as suitable for playing in the madhya kāla) in a long drawn out tempo is to commit aesthetic mutilation of the piece. So also in vocal rendering relative speeding up may be needed, while some shine best if the speed is slackened. The proper understanding of a sāhitya depends on the correct assessment of the kālapramāṇa to be utilised. Subtler and deeper aspects could be emphasised by fixing the appropriate tempo.

There is an 'art of listening' which is least taught or studied. It is not a rare or special privilege but a natural inheritance of every one who has an ear enough to distinguish one tune from another and wit enough to prefer order to incoherence. The listeners are expected to make an attempt to cultivate the art of listening and forge a close link between them and the performer, in order to get the maximum joy from the creation which has music value.

The 'concert' in the Indian context would bring to mind a group of three or four performers improvising the melody of a rāga and the rhythmic pattern of a tāḷa. Rāga and tāḷa in a sense are partial compositions. Everything depends on the technical training and the aesthetic sense of the performer that is his potential for improvisation with rāga, tāḷa and his talent. There is little in the mind of an Indian listener of contemplating eternal or static perfection. The concert of a musician is not a strain to retell. It is an attempt to express feelings at a given moment which are expressible within the grammar of a rāga and tāḷa. Thus the composer and performer are one. In other words, the audience finds itself in direct confrontation with the artiste in the heat of creation.

The word 'emotion' is a psychological pointer. To communicate emotion is not a sign of value, but an item necessary for achieving maximum communication effect. Hence the need for distinguishing between 'musical semantics' and 'aesthetic value proper' is very desirable. There seems to be an inevitable gap (at least suggestive) between 'musical content' and 'aesthetic value' itself. Value becomes relativised according to familiar patterns of renderings. This results in an expression of this or that 'pattern of rendering'. An ideological evaluation of the pattern of rendering is often attempted. All such models are however retrospective, at best they grasp an achieved work.

Musical knowledge can be acquired by self-effort and musical appreciation has to be cultivated. The emotional or aesthetic feeling associated with certain rāgas stand out and distinguished from the background of feelings. This is the reason why an uninitiated listener feels that certain rāgas are pleasing and others are not so to him. At this stage of cognition the listener will not be able to analyse what constitutes a 'Rāgaswarūpa' though he could have known the name of the rāga. He learns to identify the rāga that are consistent in compositions though he has not acquired 'svaragñāna' The names enable him to recognise and to a certain extent classify the rāgas too. He picks up the capacity to appreciate rāgas say like Kīrvāṇi, Bairavī, Karahanapriyā—all differing only at one vital point. When he hears rāgas like Ābhōgi, Śrīrañjanī and Jeganmōhinī, he may even differentiate them from portions of Manoharī and Nārāyaṇī. The knowledge that the differences lie in Ma, Da, Sa; Pa, Da, Sa; and Ni, Da, Sa; comes to him at a later stage. When he hears some unfamiliar phrases in any of the rāgas, he might say 'Oh, this is like Śrīrañjanī etc.' He might be misled into thinking that he had diagnosed it correctly. In musicacme in the art of identification is to be learnt and not acquired instantaneously. One could recognise the sharp and two flat riṣabas, for example, Nāṭa and Gauḷa; then the completely coalescing notes such as 'pa' (true fifth), çatuśṛuti Ṛṣbha (major tone); aṅtara gāṅdhāra (harmonic major third) and so on. By continued listening he could recognise harmonic notes like 'Śūdda madhyama' (perfect fourth); triśṛuti dhaivata (harmonic major sixth) and also extensible notes such as Śuraṭi Ni, Bēgaḍa Ma, etc. These will become intelligible within the framework of the rāga. Recognition, if sung separately would be possible with efflux of time. When 'svargñāna' and 'rāga gñāna' are well established, with the rāgaswarūpa well understood, the listener will be able to locate 'mūrçhanas', etc., and the rāgas relating to the shifting of the key. To know not by theory but by actual experience that Mohanam, Śuddasāvēri, Udayaraviçaṅdrika, Hiṅdōḷam and Madhyamāvati are ultimately one and the same (scale not ragas) is the acme of musical perception and enjoyment.

We are not therefore surprised when a Westerner makes the following remarks about Indian concerts: "...The Indian audience has different attitudes towards listening than does the Western audience. Indians listen intensely and analytically. Many keep time during the performance by clapping their palms on the knees and making gestures as the performer reaches 'sam' (the first beat of the tāḷa or rhythmic cycle)...when they listen they listen intensely; but when they get bored they talk or look around or even leave their seat in the middle of a performance...The behaviour of an Indian audience at a concert can be fruitfully compared to that of the audience at a sports event. By demonstration of delight, the audience encourages the performers while they are performing (every performance has a certain amount of show off or acrobatic passage which are followed by bouts of applause or signs of appreciation such as wagging the head, sighing, etc.)...The artistic success of an Indian concert therefore depends, in part, on the aesthetic level of the audience."[8]

Some art-lovers at times have felt that the standard of Carnātic music has not been maintained as before.[9] Standard of music could be measured only by quality and not quantity. Since music is a creative art it lends itself only to the qualitative analysis. When we speak of quality it is the creative aspect of this art-form. Quality implies that music ought not to be recitative, repetitive, and reproductive. In a three hour concert about twenty compositions are used and these include miscellaneous heterogeneous items. If creative aspect of music is to be emphasised large number of compositions cannot be accommodated in a concert. The time available to prove the creative ability of the artiste is reduced.

It is said that about forty years ago the piece-de-resistance in a concert was the Rāgam, Tānam and Pallavī. 'Pallavī' also described as 'Manodharma Saṅgita' calls for creative skill and mastery over rhythm. It is 'measured music' and compliments rāga ālāpana. It is claimed that Śārṅgadeva's work 'Sangītaratnākaram', Pallavī or its equivalent is described as 'Rūpālāpti' (elaboration of the image of a rāga). It had been the practice to make the opening line of a composition for elaboration. Since 1929 a controversy rages on the merits and demerits of singing elaborate Pallavīs in a concert. Until 1920's, the Pallavī seems to have been considered the 'main item' in a concert. The importance of a Pallavī as a musical form cannot be denied.[10] The question of 'the place of Pallavī in a concert' arises from the fallacy that scholarliness in a performer is to be found only in Pallavī singing. It appeals to reason that if concerts are to entertain or ennoble, they are not the forums for overelaboration of anything. Legitimately one can expect that there must be an outer covering of emotion even in the intellectual portion of a performance. It is here that 'aesthetics' asserts itself—appeal to the heart triumphs over appeal to the intellect. To ensure the balance, the primary emphasis has to be 'perspective magnitude' and 'proper proportion.'

Some artistes specialised in the handling of particular rāgas. In the past we hear of many who claimed a particular rāga as his forte. If a creative musician handles the same composition or melody at different performances, he could present something fresh. Without changing the set up very much the artiste must have had the potential to stimulate fresh emotions and sentiments. Thus new cadences of movement were created in respect of a same composition. Colloquially this is spoken of as 'way of presentation'.

To maintain 'standards' the following are often recommended: (a) The singer must have a musical voice, (b) The accompanists must give due respect to 'delicate subtlety' for which our music is famous. Excessive display is deemed unaesthetic, (c) Art must be set in artistic background. To accommodate talents at all levels, performances may be of different kinds, namely, orthodox pattern, short-duration, demonstration-concerts, etc.

Light music claimed as a distinct variety had sprung into prominence in recent years. Classification and the process of composition are to be taken into consideration. Every Indian art is the product of an indigenous tradition. Different types are included in Indian music and they are classified as tribal, folk, light-classical and classical. They have run concurrently as distinct streams and they have sustained themselves as such, since they are offshoots of a common tree. They are held together by a vital link. The various streams must have made a substantial contribution to the resources from which classical music must have been evolved, elaborated and built as a system. Various regions are known for certain unique music forms. Such music forms have great antiquity and are part of the tradition of the respective regions. (Deśi) The point that is yet to be clarified is whether such formats are products of preferential demands from a community or a cultural group.

'Creativity' is implicit in the conception of the art of composition. Is light-music a product of creative endeavour? Light music freely draws inspiration from classical music. Of late it has not been able to resist the influence of the west and Screen music. Arbitrary adoption of crescendo ending, orchestral interludes with patches of harmony introduced between the lines of singing and staccato or jazzy rhythm; have certainly detracted the integrity and beauty of native flavour.

Folk-music makes a continual interaction of cultural forces between the 'classes and the masses.' The compass of a folk-melody is generally limited to an octave or even less. This precludes the possibility of the full contour of the rāga being perceived. A folk-singer, is not bound by the variety of Gamakas. (ornamentations). The technical excellence of 'classical music' is patent. Simplicity and suggestiveness which are the essence of art are virtues which adorn folk-art. The melodies of folk-music in Tamil Nadu are conceived, remembered, and expressed musically. In non-rhythmic renderings like 'Temmāṅgu', musical expression (emotion) is striking.

In folk-music, the heptatonic scale is sparsely used. If an over-all view is taken, all the twelve 'notes' (svarasthānas) of an octave are employed. 'Pratimadhyama' is rare and this is the reason for some researchers concluding that this 'note' is absent in folk-music.[11] Harikambhoti and Śaṅkarābharaṇam seem to be the favourite mélas. (Harikāmboti=Sempālai Śaṅkarābharaṇam=Kodipālai). 'Modal shift' had been followed in Tamil Iśai. (Kural tiripu). This practice is combined with shades of consonance and assonance (Samvādi and Anuvādi) and provide the basic musical experience.

In some of the rāgas in use like Navarōj, Ceṅçurutti, Kuraṅci, Ānaṅdabhairavī, and Punnākavarāli, the influence of the folk-melody can be traced.[12] Treatment of 'notes' however registers difference. The 'notes' are slightly higher or lower in value than their counterpart in classical usage. 'Kāvaṭi çiṅtu' which often figured as one of the items of agenda in classical music performance of yesteryears, baffles analysis.[13] The 'Varṇamettūs' are unique combinations of melodic structure and rhythmic pattern. By and large, rhythm is more fixed in folk-music than in art-music. Çaturaśra and Tiśra gatis have been used profusely. In chronologically later compositions like those of Tyāgarāja, Gopālakrsna Bhrati, Ramaswāmī Śivan and few others, folk melodies have been immortalised.

Folk-rhythm commands attention. The 'Āti-tāla' (four or eight unit intervals) is supposed to be universal. In folk-songs we find frequent use of the seven unit tāḷas. (Miśra çāpu or Tripuṭa) The 'Tiśra ēka' comes second (including Rūpaka). The number seven is customarily believed to be a 'Mystic-number'. We have seven days in a week, seven sages (Sapta ṛṣis), seven 'notes' in musical scales; lunar phenomenon depends on the number seven; certain diseases are believed to assume critical stages on days which depend on number seven and so on. It is interesting to find that devotional songs (identical songs in Śṛṅgāra rasa too) are set in miśra çāpu (Triputa). Most of the Tamil hymns of saints (Tēvāram, Tiruvōimoli) lend themselves naturally to this variety of rhythm. Most of the Padas of Kṣētragña are set in Triputai tāla. These facts suggest that 'Love and Devotion' (sublimated love) are fundamental human emotions afforded by 'Nature'. Tunes of folk forms may not confine to lakṣāṇas (canon) but they are not lacking in aesthetic quality. It looks as if the very charm and appeal are due to this apparent disregard to technical requirements.

Nowadays we hear statements like Carnātic music has entered the critical phase of its history. Is this a symptom of crisis? If that be so, is it due to the impatience of the academically educated or conservative public? Or Is it due to the inability of the artistically unresponsive classes to keep pace with the avant grade !

It is difficult to define art logically. Scholars seem to be satisfied with the dictum 'Art is what counts as art'. 'Artistic structures' are concepts. The gap between aesthetic and other conscious contents is always there. This space is often divorced from practice. It is still in touch with it in many ways. If the quality of stimulation to aesthetic experience is not tampered with, it survives. We can only talk of a definitive end of art. But this may loose its utility if we think we can solve the problems by other means. The most revolutionary innovations of one period may quickly degenerate into the most insipid conventions of the next.

Every style, every movement in taste begins with the struggles against the principles of form and the concept of 'Beauty' of the preceding period. The present scenario of Carnātic music is taken as the 'legacy of the Great-age'. Overcoming the norms of certain traditions is an unquestionable condition for artistic progress. But the total rejection of tradition and conventions would mean the end of the art. When readymades are introduced into the art, it results in confusion, often enraging the listener. We are reminded that 'Everything is not art which counts as art or which it proclaims itself to be art.' Sincerity is not an aesthetic but a moral and romantic concept. The abandoning of cheap effects in art, points to the seriousness with which its adequate reception is linked. It adds to the shock-effect which moves the listener to look at the work from a new and more instructive viewpoint. This effect rarely comes without certain amount of bold experimentation and without diverging from the usual and generally accepted order of things.

Carnātic music as it stands today is to be regarded in part 'as its own denial'; that is as a phenomenon which has at the same time positive and negative elements. Even what is artistically negative, what seems to have changed qualitatively into 'Science' or 'Pseudo science' moves insofar as it has effect upon our minds—in more or less unmistakable aesthetic categories. Perhaps the claim that 'It is not the performer who fails, but history which fails' seeks justification under this premise. 'Aesthetic distance' gets reduced when objectivity and subjectivity draw closer. A work of art which breaks away from tradition is something 'objective' and when creative intention directs the display it is 'subjective'. When both blend 'aesthetic distance' becomes untenable.

Sergei Prokofiv makes the following observations. He is not referring to Carnātic music, but his observations on music have universal application. "The time is past when music was written for a handful of aesthetics. Today...people have come face to face with serious music and are waiting with eager impatience...Performers take heed of this—if you repel these crowds they would turn away from you to vulgar music... but this is not to mean that you should pander to the audience. Pandering always has a sense of insincerity about it and nothing good ever came of that. I consider it as a mistake for a performer to strive for simplification. Any attempt to 'play down' to the listener is a subconscious underestimation of his cultural maturity and the development of his tastes...music that is insincere cannot be enduring...let us learn to appreciate really good music... And what is good music? Not cheap little tunes that sound nice when you first hear them but which you soon get tired of, but melodies that have their roots in classical music and in folk-songs. But why classical and folk music are considered as good music? Because that music had stood the test of time, it had lived for tens and even hundreds of years and still gives us pleasure."[14]

The modern phase of classical Carnātic music started off well. Happy exceptions apart the modern trend ignores 'Rakti' or aesthetic delight. The world in which it thrives euphemistically describes it as 'Intellectual'. There is a patent imbalance or needless aggression allround. The preceding generation largely employed essential elements namely dynamic music intervals (svaras) which are different from 'note-positions', euphonious words as distinguished from bizarre sounds and gentle rhythm as opposed to aggressive percussion.

Music-critic is a conspicuous figure in the concert halls of today. The purpose as I see it, on the one hand is evaluation, what may be called 'providing value judgement'. On the other it is to propagate or widen 'aesthetic education.' Those who are uninitiated, those who are fresh listeners may seek to find an element of aesthetic education too. In a 'concert', there is a communicator and a recipient. In terms of his own perception, the sensation is interpreted. What is heard is interpreted (in the mind) in terms of the artistic values which the individual listener had achieved or acquired. To this extent, it is subjective. Everyone has areas of likes, dislikes, prejudices and built in resistance.

D.H. Lawrence had made certain observations pertaining to literary criticism which are applicable to art-criticism in a broader sense. "...Criticism can never be a science; it is in the first place much too personal and in the second is concerned with values that science ignores. The touchstone is *Emotion, not Reason*. We judge a work of art by its effect on our sincere and vital emotion and nothing else. All the critical twiddle-twiddle about style and form, all the pseudo-scientific classification and analysis in an imitation botanical fashion, is mere impertinence and most dull jargon...A critic must be able to feel the impact of a work of art in all its complexity and force. To do so, he must be a man of force and complexity himself, which few critics are. A man with a paltry, impudent nature will never write anything but paltry, impudent criticism. A man who is emotionally educated is rare as a phoenix."[15]

The growth of the function and reputation of the critic is a sign not only of the commercialisation of the press, but also of the democratisation and levelling out of the public. The part that a critic plays in the aesthetic education is obvious; what is questionable is whether he exerts an educative influence upon the artiste and influences the directions of his creations. The artiste scarcely ever becomes converted by criticism into a new artistic volition. So criticism is least intended to the artiste. When it addresses him with objections, advice and directives ; it is felt superflous. The artiste creates and his ability to create embraces his competence to evaluate them adequately. This is really 'self-examination'and not 'criticism'. The artiste's particular interest, his prejudices conditioned by rivalry, his one sided sensibility may even impair his judgement. The most serious objection to this 'self-assessment' is, it makes the overcoming of technical difficulties a criterion of artistic worth and disregards the significance of effortless or spontaneous creativity.

Radio and television developed into mass media. They cater to the normal scheme of things with their fixed schedules and serialisations. Even the trimmings of the main course change according to an inevitable menu. In all these there are two different varieties of products which have different aims : (a) Those which are devoted to information and teaching and (b) those which serve entertainment or a preferred artistic end. The 'artistic value' is often problematical. The choice of programmes are relatively limited, more or less organised on the same lines, so that the critical listener who does not wish to see or hear can do nothing but to turn off his set.

Radio is a thoroughly ambivalent medium. Its ambivalence begins with the fact that its didactic value is just as indisputable as the nature of its artistic significance appears problematic. The simultaneous good and ill which it does is most clearly seen in music. Radio brings much music to the public by enabling people to hear them in the comfort of the house. But it robs them of the means by which they can test the suitability of their musical ear. It is true that the programmes of the mass media are intended for a large number of consumers, but not necessarily for a public which listen to the programme enmasse. People have talked about end of art as something in the immediate future or indeed as something which had already begun. The difference is that up to the introduction of the Radio (later television) people were thinking of the end of a certain period, movement or function of art, of one of its heydays or otherwise decisive epochs. It is only since the introduction of the radio that people have begun talking about the collapse of art and a symptom of total cultural development which has apparently come to an end.

The problem is to be viewed from the point of view of the inhibiting effect of name-myths on the climate of listening. Consequently, the chances of rise of fresh talents demand attention. Bias for or against names cannot be eliminated in music-hall performances too. In their broadcast of music programmes let the All India Radio announce the names of the artistes at the conclusion of the programme only. In the advance publicity through dailies and periodicals, programmes are to be distinguished by numbers. Subsequent issues may carry the names of musicians with particulars of date, programme number and artiste. The All India Radio is the largest single employer and publicity medium. No wonder teachers train the pupils to meet this ill-conceived demand.

What is it that the audition boards expect? It is the singing of the 'kalpana svara' even for the entrants! 'Kalpana svaras' have artistic values only when they come out with natural ease and maturity. A thirty-minute performance by a B-grade artiste will certainly not suffer for lack of 'svara singing'. Since All India Radio requires it is mechanically drilled. Many good voices have been spoiled and classical music itself has come into disrepute. This mishap may be overcome if sensible criteria are laid down. Pleasing tone-production and classical rendering of first-rate compositions may be expected from the entrant. At higher levels Kalpana svara, Rāgālāpana and Niraval may form the criteria.

It is difficult to propose a worthwhile thesis on the nature of art without getting involved in contradictions. The emotion of art is impersonal. Significance of form and content, purposeful or purposeless beauty, spontaneous and conventional modes of expression, historically concrete and artistic motifs which are separate from history are not mutually exclusive. Therefore no mistake is committed if we see in the paradoxical, the reconciliation of the incompatible—a fundamental form of art. Ultimately, we understand by aesthetics a change of criteria of taste, concepts of beauty and conceptions of form.

REFERENCES

1. *B.C. Deva* : Psycho-accoustics of Music and Speech (The Music Academy, 1967).
2. *B.C. Deva* : The Vibrato in Indian Music (Acoustica-9, 1951), pp. 175-90.
3. *B.C. Deva* : Traditional elements in Music. (Nada-rupa, January 1963), p. 44ff.
4. Geetam vādyōbyam yatra Saṅgīta iti uçyatē.
5. Gīta-vādya pada nyāsanam

   krya-ka-layō: parasparam samata.
6. The treatise Saṅgīta Dāmōdara (1653 A.D.) since listing the defects of a vocalist includes 'Talaheena' and 'Layasthanavivarjitam' (Chapter III). The work is authored by Dāmōdara Misra, son of Lakṣmīdhara. He tried to co-ordinate theory and tradition known up to his time.
7. Talāntra vartya : kālōyam laya naka.
8. Jerry Cohn: A Westerner looks at Indian concert. (Indian Music Journal, (ed) V.V. Sadagopan, 1966, April-May), pp. 45-46.
9. R.Srinivasan : Let us face facts. (Indian Music Journal, *op. cit.*), p. 31.
10. V. Gomathi Sankara Iyer : Mahāvaidyanāta Śivan (Tamil) Parts I & II (Chidambaram).
11. Shyāmaḷa Bālakrishnan : Folk Music of Tamil Nadu vis-a-vis Classical Carnatic Music (Indian Music Journal, *op. cit.*, Nos. 13-14, 1971), p. 25

    Differs from the popular view and states that 'there is a conjunction of Prati and Śudda madhyamas... a case of seepage from an ancient classical melody.
12. *Ibid.*
13. Kāvati cintu : Supra. Chapters III and V.
14. S. Prokofiev : Autobiography etc.; (Foreign Languages Publishing House, Moscow).
15. There is a Sanskrit saying 'Pāndityám nividya bālyēṇa tistāseth' (Forget all your scholastic learning, try to sit, listen like a child in wonder).

Appendix

LAKSANA GRANTHAS

1. *Bharata's Nāṭyaśāstra.* : (Sanskrit) Many editions.
2. *Nārada Śikṣā*: (Gaekwad Oriental Series, Sanskrit).
3. *Dattilam* : (Dattila muni, Mukund Lath, Implex, India 1978, New Delhi).
4. *Bṛhaddēśī* : (Mataṅga, Sanskrit, Trivandrum Library).
5. *Saṅgīta Makaraṅda of Nārada* : (Sanskrit series).
6. *Saṅgīta Sudhākara* : (Haripāla, 12th C. A.D.).
7. *Saṅgīta Samayasāra* : (Sanskrit, Pārśvadēva, 1165 to 1330 A.D.).
8. *Mānasōllāsa* : (A.D. 1130 also known as Abilāṣārtha Ċintāmāṇi Sōmēśvara (?) Çālūkya. A.D. 1130).
9. *Saṅgīta Sāra* : (Vidyāraṇya. Gōviṅda Dēśikar refers to the work, 14th C. A.D.).
10. *Saṅgītōupaniṣadsārōddara* : (A.D. 1350. Sudā kalasa. Jain).
11. *Saṅgītaratnākaram* : (Śārṅgadēva. 13th century A.D.) Patronised by Yādava kings. Well-known Sanskrit treatise on music. The best commentary on the work is by Çaturakaḷḷinātha (Kalānidi). Another commentary is by king Simhabhūpāla. (Only portions of svarādhyāya are available) A third commentary is by king Kumbakarṇa of Mewar. Another, commentary is Saṅgītaratnākara Çandrikā (Author not known Ref : Volume I Catalogue of Sanskrit Mss. in South India No. 6258) other commentaries are by Kesavan a brahmin. A Hindi commentary ('Sētu' by Gaṅgārām, T.M.S.S.M. Library, Thanjore. 6598(a). A metrical work is available in Tamil (Catalogue of Tamil books. T.M.S.S.M. Library, Thanjore, No. 634 B).

12. *Rāgārṇava* : Author not known. May be dated 14th C.A.D. could be earlier than A.D. 1330.
13. *Saṅgītārnava* : The work is quoted in the context of Dance Ref : Saṅgītasaṅgraha-Çiṅtāmani. (Adayar-Library).
14. *Gōpāla Nāyaka* : (1295 to 1315 A.D.) Perhaps, Gōpāla Nāyaka was called Çaturdaṇḍi.
15. *Saṅgīta Sudhākara* : Haripāla dēva 1309 to 1312 A.D. The author is said to be a Yādava ruler of Devagiri. (?)
16. *Saṅgīta Sāra* :Vidyāraṇya 1320 to 1380 A.D.
17. *Saṅgita Vidyā Vinōda* : Earlier than fourteenth century.
18. *Bharata Saṅgraha* : Vidyāçakravartin. Beginning of the fourteenth century A.D.
19. *Rājakandarbha* : Author not known. Quoted by Mallinātha. Ref : Kālidāsa's Kumārasambava).
20. *Saṅgīta Çiṅtāmaṇi* : Vēmabhūpāla. Commencement of the fifteenth century. The king is also known as Vīranārāyana KOMATI (?) He is said to be belonged to Kodaivīdu and patron of Vāmana Bhatta-Bāṇa.
21. *Saṅgīta* : Kamala loçana. Ref : Aufrecht's. *Ciṅtāmaṇi Saṅgītāmṛta.* catalogue. K.96 (Keilhorn's catalogue).
22. *Ānaṅda Saṅjīvana* : Rāja Madanapāla. Earlier than 1528 A.D. (Bikaner Catalogue. Ms 1090) p. 509
23. *Saṅgīta Sarvōdaya* : Lakṣmīnārāyaṇa. First quarter of the sixteenth century. Introductory verses describe the city of Vyāpuri (Vijayanagar). Author's guru is given as Viṣṇu Bhattāraka. A Rājavākgēyakāra. (royal musician) (Ref : Madras Government Oriental Manuscript Library Triennial Catalogue 1922-23 to 1924-25 R. 4516).
24. *Rāgadīpikā* : Must be dated earlier than 16th century A.D.
25. *Rāgalakṣmī Vilāsa* : Laksmīdhara. Sṛtiranjani quotes this.
26. *Vāmadēveeyam* : Quoted in Lakṣmīdharā's Śṛutiranjani deals with a dance caraṅá.
27. *Bharataśāstra graṅtha* : Çārukavi Lakṣmīdhara. 16th C. A.D. (Bhandarkar Institute Library. The work deals with Nāṭya and Saṅgīta).
28. *Gīta Prakāśa* :First half of the 16th century. (Madras Mss . Library, Script in the Oriya language).

29. *Svaramelakalānidhi :* Rāmamātya 1550 A.D. Contemporary of Rāmarāya of Vijayanagar. (M.S. Ramaswami Iyer. Annamalai University). Three editions of the work—an old South-Indian edition; an edition with Marāti notes by Bathkaṇde; and Annamalai University edition by M.S. Ramaswami Iyer.
30. *RāgamālāRāgamañjarī Sadrāga Caṅdrōdaya :* Pundarīka Vittala. Vittala belongs to the village of Satanūrva near the hill Śivagaṅga in Karnātaka. A brahmin of the Jamatagnya Vamśa (Karnātaka-Jātiya). Viṭṭala flourished in the court of Burhan Khan of Pharaki family (1370 to 1600 A.D.) at a city Ānaṅdavalli in Kāndēs in the south. Rājamāla has an earlier vernacular version called Sugama-Rājamāla written by Kalyāṇa Kavi. Rājamaṅjarī praises Akbar under whom were two brothers Mādhava Simha and Māna Simha kings of 'Kaççapa Vamśa'. Two more works namely Nṛtyanirṇaya and Saṅgītanṛtyaratnākara are attributed to Viṭṭala.
31. *Rāgavibhōda :* Sōmanātha. Marāti gloss in print available. English translation of the work is popular in the West. (K.B. Deval Theory of Indian Music as expounded by Sōmanātha). M.S. Rāmaswāmi Iyer has edited the work with an English translation. Internal evidence provides Śāka 1531 or A.D. 1609 as date of composition. (at the end of the work) Deccan college manuscript (XIXI Ms no. 276) speaks of Rāgavibōdavivēka and describes it as a commentary on Rāgavibhōda.
32. *Sangīta Sarvasva :* Jagaddara. Could be placed between fourteenth and seventeenth centuries.
33. *Tānappaçārya :* (A.D. 1600) is mentioned in Veṅkaṭamakin's Çaturdaṇḍi prakāśika'. Saṅgīta Sampradāya Pradarśini of Eṭṭayāpuram mentions him as a northerner and guru of Veṅkaṭamakin. (Outtaradēśika) Some scholars identify him with Tān-Ussain of the court of emperor Akbar. Çaturdaṇḍi mentions him as 'Paramā guru'. P.S. Sundaram Iyer of Tanjore held the view that Tānappa is Veṅkaṭamakin's father Gōvinda Dīkṣita. (Journal of the Madras Music Academy, Vol II. 3), p. 154. Saṅgīta Sūḍā, the work of Gōvinda Dīkṣita makes no mention of Tānappa. Anupa Simha, king of Bikaner (1671 to 1709 A.D.) in his work Anupa-Saṅgīta mentions that he is the grandson of Tāna Bhatta. Is he to be identified with Tānappa?

34. *Sangīta Sūda* : Gōvinda Dīksita, A.D. 1614. King Reghunātha Nāyak of Tanjore is sometimes spoken of as the author. (Ref : P.S. Subramanya Śāstri, Journal of the Madras Music Academy, Vol II, No. 1). Gōvinda Dīksita is also known as Ayyan. Historical prelude of seventy-seven verses of the work is valuable to the historian. The language (Sanskrit) is exquisite.
35. *Çaturdaṇḍiprakāsika* : Veṅkaṭamakin alias Veṅkaṭadvāri (A.D. 1620) -Veṅketēśvara Dīkṣita is the son of Gōvinda-Dīksita. (The work published by the Music Academy, Madras) A Telugu version of the work procured from Eṭṭayāpuram was made use of by T.L. Veṅkaṭarama Iyer and rendered in Sanskrit. Bhatkande published portions of the work (taken from Telugu Mss). In the work Veṅkaṭamakin claims that he devised seventy-two meḷakarta scheme that is absolutely above reproach and that not even God Śīva could improve on it. (Méḷādvi Saptāti. Śrīmad Veṅkaṭadvāri Kalpita, etc.) As currently available the work does not contain the end of the penultimate chapter and the entire last chapter. End of eleventh chapter (Prabaṅdhas) and twelfth chapter (tāḷas) are lost. Rāmamātya author of Svaramēḷakalānidi is spoken of with contempt. According to Subramania sastrikal of Tanjore 'Çaturdaṇḍi' refers to four forms of singing namely Gīta, Prabandha, Tāya, and Alāpa. Rāmakrṣṇa Kavi says that the word 'Çaturdaṇḍi' occurs in early works and means four parts of a Rāga: Stāyi, Sancāri, Ārōha, and Avarōha. Veṅkaṭamakin has composed Lakṣaṇa gitas printed in Sampradāyapradarśini.
36. *Saṅgīta Darpaṇa* : Dāmōdara. (A.D. 1625) son of Lakṣmīdara Bhatta. Had the title 'Çatura' like Kallināta. Work based on Sōmanāta's Rāga-Vibōda.
37. *Saṅgīta Darpaṇa* : Haribhatta. (Bikaner Catalogue Ms. no. 1123, p. 527. Oppert's catalogue and Burnell's at Tanjore describe a work called Saṅgīta Sārōddāra by Haribhatta. This work is available in Madras Mss Library too) Saṅgīta-Darpaṇa of Dāmōdara does not contain a separate section on Drvas. Saṅgīta Sārōddara has a section on Dṛvas.
38. *Saṅgīta Kalānidhi* : Haribhatta (Aufrecht's catalogue).
39. *Saṅgīta Sāroddara* : Kīkarāja, son of Sajjana (Aufrecht) also (Bhandarkar Oriental Institute, Poona, No. 838 of 1886-92).
40. *Saṅgīta Çandra* : Abilash.

41. *Saṅgīta Bhāskara :* King Jegajyōtirmalla. (1617 to 1635 A.D.) Jegajyōtirmalla is a Nepalese king (A.D. 1617 to 1633) M.M. Haraprasad-Śāstri informs us that Abhilāsha composed Saṅgīta Çandra while at South India and that the king took it to Nepal even as 'Garuda brought Amṛta'. The work treats 'Nāṭya' elaborately. The work is in prose and verse and has a commentary(Saṅgīta Bhāskara) by Vāngamani a court poet of the Nepalese king and a native of Mithila.
42. *Saṅgīta Sāra Samgraha :* Author king Jegajyōtirmalla. A work in prose and verse. Deals with music, dance and drama. (Nepalese catalogue. Nepalese Palace Library) The king is also the author of an opera 'Hara-Gaurī-Vivāha' in Nepalese dialect.
43. *Saṅgīta Pārijāta :* Ahōbala (17th century) published from Bengal. Refers to many ancient writers on music. Bases the text on Hanuman's work. It is claimed that the work was translated into Persian in A.D. 1724.
44. *Saṅgita Makaraṅda Saṅgīta Puṣpānjali :* Vēda. Work as stated in the Bikaner. catalogue speaks only of Nṛtyādyaya. But copies available at Tanjore (Burnel catalogue, p. 60 a) suggests more chapters on music. Saṅgīta-Makaraṅda treats Rasadṛṣtis, Gatīs cāris, Hastas, various dances and rasas. Patron of the author is 'Shahu'. The work gives the patron's vamśāvaḷi. (geneology). It belongs to the early part of the 17th century. Names of two musicians (Gōpāla and Ambapurī) are mentioned. S.R. Bhandarkar's Ms (catalogue of Rajasthan and Central Asia) informs that Vēda is the son of Āmaṅda, the son of Dāmōdara. If this is admitted Vēda is the grandson of the author of Sangīta Darpaṇa.
45. *Saṅgīta Kalpataru :* Author not ascertainable. Work resembles Nātyaśāstra of Bharata. Date could be assigned as earlier to 1655 A.D. Rāya Gaṇeśa dēva wrote a commentary (Subōdhini) patronised by a king Khadgabāhu son of Vīrasimha.
46. *Rāgataraṅgiṇi Rāga Saṅgīta-Saṅgraha :* A.D. 1700.- Lōçana-Kavi. Rāgataraṅgiṇi is a work on Hindustani music. Author is a native of Mithila and styles himself 'Svadēśa'. A small work dealing with rāgas prescribes appropriate time for singing each rāga (Rāgānām gānakāla: Tumburu nāṭakē) Perhaps the only source that gives the name of Tumburu as Tumburu-Nāṭaka.

Internal evidence provides Śaka 1082 (A.D. 1160). This Śaka is not the well-known Salivāhana era but appears to be some local era. Rāja Sangīta Sangraha is another work of Lōçana.

47. *Rāgatatva Vibhōda* : Śrīnivāsapandita. Latter half of the seventeenth century. Contains a discussion on the ethics of music.

48. *Hṛdayaprakāśa. Mṛdanga kautuka* : King Hṛdayanārāyaṇa. A.D. 1667 ruler of 'Gatandurga' (Jubbalpore' (A.D. 1667.) The works are short and deal with rāgas only.

49. *Rāgamañjarī* : These three works are quoted by *Rāgakutūhalam Rāgakautukam* Bhāva Bhatta. Details about contents are not ascertainable.

50. *Anūpa Sangīta-Vilāṣa, Anūpa Sangīta ratnakara and Anūpa Saṅgīta aṅkuśa.* : These three works are assigned to King Anupa, Bhāva Bhatta. King Anupasimha is the patron of Bhāva Bhatta, ruler of Bikaner (1674 to 1709 A.D.) Bhāva Bhatta is the son of Sangīta Rāya Janārdana Bhatta court-musician of the emperor Shahjéhan. Ankuśa has two chapters one on Svara and another on Rāga. Rāga chapter is called Ālāpana-mañjari. Anūpa Sangīta Ratnākara has chapters on Svara and Rāga. It borrows heavily from other works like those of Śārngadeva. Anūpa Sangīta Vilāśa refers to rāga Atāna and the author claims that the statements about the rāga are his own. (Iyam-Madukti). This work has three chapters Śruti, Svara and Rāga. Other unpublished/partially published works of Bhāva Bhatta are Sangīta Vinōda, Mṛaliprakāśa, Nastōdistaprabhōdaka Draupada teeka (treatise on Drupad singing).

51. *Śivatatva Ratnākara* : Basava Rāja or Basappa king of Kēladi dynasty said to have ruled for two hundred and fifty years, (1698 to 1715 A.D.) In this encyclopaedic work three chapters (VII to IX) deal with music (Svara; Rāga, Tāla). Chapter VII deals with Nāda, Svara, Grāma, Mūrcana, Alankāra and Gamaka. Chapter VIII deals with Jātis and Rāgas and closes with Gāyalaksanam chapter IX covers Tāla and Vādya.

52. *Saṅgīta Sārāmṛta* : King Tulaja. An epitome of the work has been published from Bombay.

53. *Saṅgīta Śāstra Sānkṣēpa* : 18th century work authored by Gōvinda. Original manuscript is in the Telugu language. Difficult

to fix the exact date of the work. Upper limit can be fixed as during the reign period of Açyuta Nāyak (1577 to 1614 A.D.). Opinions differ as to whether the work is pre-Veṅkatamakin or post-Veṅkatamakin. Ramakṛṣṇa Kavi claims that Govinda is an Andradēśi. There is reference to an anonymous work Saṅgraha çūḍāmaṇi as part of Skaṅdapurāṇa.

54. *Saṅgīta Saṅgraha Çintāmāṇi :* Author Appaḷaçāri. (Adayar Mss Library XXXX) contains chapters on tāḷa and Nartana. Sanskrit verses are followed by a Tamil gloss. Appaḷāçāri is a native of Śrīmuṣṇam village near Cidambaram in Tamil Nadu. Work may be assigned to the nineteenth century.

55. *Mēḷādhikāra Lakṣaṇa :* Anonymous work in music found in T.M.S.S. Mahal Library, Tanjore. T.L. Venkatarama Iyer assigns the work to early eighteenth century. (Journal of the Madras Music Academy, Volume I, No. 1). The work gives twenty-four Srutis.

56. *Saṅgīta Dāmōdarā :* Dr. Keith refers to the work. (Sanskrit drama) deals with music and dance.

57. *Saṅgīta Kaumudī :* (Trienniel catalogue. Oriental Ms Library, Madras 1922-23; 1924-25 R. 4163) King Sanasena (?) is said to be the author.

58. *Saṅgīta Nārāyaṇa :* King Nārāyana of Paralakimēdi (Kimundi line) Utkal (Orissa) (Madras Mss Library, Triennial catalogue 1919-20, 1921-22 R.No. 3234; 1922-25 R. 4212) Work in four chapters, (a) Nāda, Śruti, Svara, Grāma, Rāga, Gīta, and Tāḷa, (b) Vādya, (c) Nṛtya (d) Prabaṅdhas. Number of works are quoted. In Rajendralal Misra's Mss of Bengal catalogues by Haraprasād Śāstri, Puruṣōttama-Kavi Ratna is mentioned as the author of the work.

59. *Alaṅkāra Çaṅdrikā:* This deals with Alaṅkāra in singing. Assigned to Nārāyaṇa. In some of the compositions the authorship mudra is of king Nārāyaṇa-Gajapati. This king belongs to the dynasty of Gaṅgas (Orissa). The title Nārāyaṇa is common to all Kimēdi chiefs and therefore it is difficult to fix the author.

60. *Saṅgīta Sāraṇi :* Poet Nārāyaṇa. (Madras Mss Library, Triennial catalogue (1919-22, R. 3298), Work is styled as 'Road to music'. Chapters are called 'Pravēśas'. (approaches). Speaks of two varieties of Prabaṅdhas namely Śudda Prabaṅdha and Sūtra

Prabandha. A Śudda Prabandha is like Gīta Govinda, several songs being set to different rāgas. The second variety is sung at the end only in a single rāga. (Sūtra Prabandha. Katita: ēkarāga nivēṣitā).

61. *Saṅgīta Sāgara :* Pratāp Sing (1779 to 1804 A.D.) Mahārāja Pratāpasimha deva of Jaipur. 'Rudra damarudbava sūtra vivaraṇam speaks of Mahesvara sūtras because they emanated from the Nāda emanated from Rudra's hand drum Damaru.
62. *Saṅgīta Śudhānidhi :* The work is mentioned in Rāghave-Bhatta's commentary on Śākuntalam (Kale's edition, p. 185).
63. *Tāladaśaprāṇadipika :* Govinda. (Ms. in Burnel's) Tanjore catalogue. A poem in Telugu in the form of songs on Śrī Rāma each song illustrative of a tāḷa. (Tāḷalakṣaṇa Mahākāvya). The work is similar to Tippa Būpāla's Tāḷaprabandha, a music composition on Śiva illustrating each tāḷa. Similarly there are Tāḷamālika compositions on one hundred and eight tāḷas of which fifty-six are available in print of Rāmaswāmī Dīkṣitar, father of Muttuswāmī Dīkṣitar.
64. *Nāṭya Cūḍāmaṇi Svararāga Śudhārasa*: Sōmanārya. Work deals with all branches of music and dance. Regarding the date we can only speculate that it is later than Rāga-Vibhōda of Sōmanātha (A.D. 1600).
65. *Tāḷa Lakṣaṇam :* Anonymous work on Tāḷa available in the Madras Library. (Decennial catalogue Volume XXII. 212993).
66. *Mṛdaṅga Lakṣaṇam :* Work on making Mṛdaṅga. Author not assignable. Decennial catalogue XXII R. 13011, R. 11 Number of works small in stature are available. Information contained in them is either repetitive or scanty. They cannot be taken serious note of. List of catalogues that could provide information.

(a) *Mss. Catalogues :* Indian and foreign.
(b) *Music manuscript works in Government Oriental Mss. Library*, Madras.
(c) *Adayar Library*, Madras.
(d) *Th anjai Mannar Serfōji Saraswati Mahāḷ Library Thanjāvūr.* (T.M.S.S.M.L.).
(e) *Bhandarkar Oriental Institute, Mss.*

Additional References

(This list excludes those mentioned in references cited in the Chapters).

Alexander, S. : *Beauty and Greatness in Art, (Aristotelian Society, 1930)*

Barton, E.H. : *A Textbook of Sound*, (London, 1922)

Bartholomew, Wilmer : *Acoustics of Music*, (New York, 1945)

Benary, B.L. : *Within the Carnātic Tradition*, (Wesleyan University, U.S.A., 1973)

Bendetto, Croce : *Aesthetics* (Tr) Douglas Ainslie, (MacMillan & Co. Ltd., 1922)

Dass, Bhagawan : *The Science of Emotion*, (Theosophical Publishing Society, Madras, 1900)

Bhathande, V.N. : *A Comparative Study of Some of the Leading Music Systems of the 15th, 16th, 17th and 18th Centuries*, (S. Lal & Co., Delhi, 1984)

Bosanquet, B. : *History of Aesthetics*, (London, 1956, Reprint)

Bullough Edward : *Aesthetics*, (London, 1957)

Chatterjee, S.K. : *Master Artist and Renovator*, Rabindranath Tagore, Golden Jubilee Volume, IISOA)

Chaudhari, P.L. : *Psychical Distance in Indian Aesthetics*, (Journal of Aesthetics and Art Criticism, London, December, 1948)

Cumaraswāmī, A.K. : *Transformation of Nature in Art,* (Dover Publication, New York, 1956).

: *The Aim of Indian Art,* (Broad Campden, 1908)

Crossley, Peler : *Artistic Values in Traditional Music,* (International Institute of Comparative Music and Documentation, Berlin, 1966)

Danielou, A. : *Introduction to the Study of Musical Scales,* (New Delhi, 1980)

Das Gupta, S.N. : *History of Indian Aesthetics I,* (England, 1949)

Dēśikar, Daṇḍāpaṇī : *Chāchapanta Venba,* (Tamil, Mayuram, 1962)

Dēva, Chaitanyam B. : *Semantic Descriptions and Synthetic Relations to Rāgas,* (Sangīt Nāṭaka Akademi, New Delhi, 1953)

Feibleman James, K. : *Aesthetics—A study of Fine-Arts in Theories and Practice,* (New York, 1970)

Franji, F. : *Bhāratīya Śṛuti, Swara and Rāga Theory,* (Āryabūshan Press, Poona, 1935)

Ganitti, E.F. : *Philosophy of Beauty,* (London, 1931)

Eueratt, Gilbert : *A History of Aesthetics,* (London, 1948)

Goswami, O. : *The Story of Indian Music,* (Asian Publishing House, 1957)

Gupta, Rakesh : *Psychological Studies in Rasa,* (Calcutta, 1950)

Havell, E.B. : *The Ideals of Indian Art,* (London, 1911)

Iyer, K. Bharath	:	(ed) *Art and Thought,* (London, 1942)
Iyengar, Śrīnivāsa, P.	:	*Saṅgītānubhava Saṅgraha, Pts. I & II (Tamil),* Madras.
Jānakīrāman, S.S.	:	*Rāga Sudarasam (Tamil),* (Author, Madras, 1970)
Jeans, Sir James	:	*Science and Music,* (ed. Cambridge, 1953)
Johnson	:	(ed) *Principles of Taste,* (1806, Third Edn.)
Khandalawala, K.	:	*A Study of Indian Painting and Music,* (Faber & Faber, London, 1953)
Knight, Murray	:	*Philosophy of the Beautiful Being: Outlines of the History of Aesthetics,* (1895)
Kramrisch, Stella	:	*Art of India through Ages,* (London, 1965)
Leistowel, Earl of	:	*A Critical History of Modern Aesthetics,* (London, 1933)
Masson, J.L. & Patavardhana M.V.	:	*Aesthetic Rapture,* Two Vols. (English Deccan College, Pune, 1970)
Mauron Charles, Roger Fry	:	(Tr) *Aesthetics and Psychology,* (London, W.C. 1935)
Menon, Rāghava R.	:	*Discovering Indian Music,* (Somaiya Publications, Bombay, 1973)
Miller, D.C.	:	*The Science of Musical Sounds,* (New York, 1922)
Mitra, Haridas	:	*Contribution to a Bibliography of Indian Art and Aesthetics,* (Visva-bharati, 1951)
Mukherjee, R.	:	*The Social Function of Art,* (Bombay, 1951)
Nettleship, R.L.	:	*On the Nature of Aesthetic Emotion,* (Mind, Vol. III, No. X, 1951)

Pandey, K.C. : *Comparative Aesthetics,* Vol. I (Banaras, 1950). *History of Indian Aesthetics,* Vol. II, (Banaras, 1952)

Rāghavan, V. : *The Number of Rasas,* (Adayar Library, Vol. 23, 1967)

Ray, Niharanjana : (ed) *Indian Aesthetics and Art Activity,* Parts I & II (Simla 1968-70)

Ravesz, G. : *Introduction to the Psychology of Music,* (London, 1953)

Sanatayana, S. : *The Sense of Beauty,* (1896)

Sahukar, Mani : *The Appeal in Indian Music,* (Thacker & Co., Bombay, 1943)

Śankar, Ravi : *Music Memory,* (Kinnara School of Music, Bombay, 1965)

Śankaran, T. : *Music Geniuses,* (Tamil, Tamil Isai Sangam, Madras, 1965)

Śarmā, Śyāmaḷa : *Aesthetics of Indian Music and Dance,* (Indian Institute of Advanced Study, Simla, 1968)

Śāstrī, P.S. : *Values and Aesthetic Experience,* (Sagar University)

Śāstrī, K.S.R. : *Indian Aesthetics,* (Madras, 1966)

The Indian Concept of the Beautiful, (Travancore, 1947)

Śāstrī, P. Pañchāpageśa : *The Philosophy of Aesthetic Pleasure,* (Annamalai University, 88, No. 6, 1940)

Śāstrī, Sāligrāma : *Sāhitya Darpana,* (Delhi, 1956)

Sen, R.K. : *Nature of Aesthetic Enjoyment in Greek and Indian Analysis,* (Seminar of Aesthetics, Simla, 1966)

Swāmi, Prajñānanda : *Historical Development of Indian Music,* (Calcutta, 1960)

Tagore, R.N. : *Creative Unity,* (London, 1922)

Toney, Donald Francis : *The Forms of Music,* (New York, 1956)

UNESCO : *The Artistes (Music) in Modern Society,* (Paris, 1952)

Viśwanāthan, R.K. : *The Physics of Music,* (Annamalai University, Annamalai Nagar, 1947)

Vivas, Elico : *Problems of Aesthetics,* (New York, 1960)

Wadiyar, Jaya Chāmarāja : *An Aspect of Indian Aesthetics,* (Madras University).

JOURNALS, BULLETINS AND DICTIONARIES

Journal of the Music Academy, Madras.

Annual Conference Souvenirs of the Music Academy, Madras. Conference Reports (Annual) of the Proceedings of the Tamil Isai Sangam, Madras.

Indian Music Journal, (Delhi Sangeetha Samaj (ed) V.V. Sadagopan) all available numbers.

Journal of the Tanjore Mannar Serfoji's Saraswathi Mahal Library.

Grove's Dictionary of Music and Musicians, (Eric Bloom, New York, 1954).

The Hindu (Weekly Magazine).

Dictionary of Music (Harvard University).

Bulletin of the Institute of Traditional Cultures (Madras-5).

Journal of the Indian Society of Oriental Art.

Glossary

Abhinayu	Expression of ideas by body and facial movements
Alaīkāras	Musical excellence in rāgas and compositions
Alpatva	Weak svaras
Anuvādī	Submedian note
Bāṣāṅga svara	Foreign note
Bhāva	Expression (lyrics)
Ḉhayālaga Rāga	Having tinge of one or two rāgas
Deśī Saṅgīta	Music of the region
Lakṣaṇa	Science or identification
Maṇipravāḷa	Mixed language
Mātrā	Time unit of tāḷa
Mūrḉhhana	A straight sequence of seven svaras
Notation	Method adopted for writing compositions
Nyāsa	Concluding portion of a svara phrase
Auḍavita	Scale having five notes in ārohaṇa and avarohaṇa (Pentatonic scale)
Pramāṇa Śṛuti	A variety of Śṛuti interval
Rasa	Taste (Normally spoken of as of nine varieties)
Samvādī	A consonant note which has concordant relationship with Vādi or tonic
Saṅkīrṇa	Complicated rāga (miśra) giving shades of more than two or three rāgas

Ṣāḍavika	Scale having six notes both in ārohaṇa and avarohaṇa.
Sthāyī	Octave or voice register consisting seven notes (Sa to Ni)
Sthāyī Bhāva	Aesthetic element underlying Navarasas

TAMIL

Ēḷu svaras	Kural (Sa), Tuttam (Ili), Kaikkilai (Ga), Uḷai (Ma), Iḷi (Pa), Viḷari (Da), Tāram (Ni)
Pālais	Caturam (4), Trikōṇam (5), Āyam (6), Vaṭṭam (7)
Yāḷ	Bēri Yāḷ (21 strings, all three stāyis), Makara (17 strings and 2½ stāyis), Sakōṭa (14 strings and 2 stāyis), Śeṅkōṭṭi (7 strings and 1 stāyi)

EQUIVALENTS I

Śempālai = Harikāmbōji; Paṭuṁpālai = Naṭabhairavī ; Kōṭippālai-Karaharapriyā; Viḷarippālai = Todī; Śevvaḷi = Śudda Tōḍī ; Aruṁpālai = Śaṅkarābharaṇam;-Mércеṁpālai = Kalyāṇī.

EQUIVALENTS II

Peruṁpaṇ = Heptatonic (7 + 7)

Paṇṇiyāl = Hexatonic (6 + 6)

Tiram = Pentatonic (5 + 5)

Tirāttiram = Quadratonic (4 + 4)

EQUIVALENTS III

	Ārohana	*Avarohana*	*Total*
Paṇ paṇṇiyal	7	6	13
Paṇ tiram	7	5	12
Paṇtirāttiram	7	4	11
Paṇniyāl paṇ	6	7	13
Paiyāl tiram	6	5	11

	Ārohana	*Avarohana*	*Total*
Paṇṇiyāl tirāttiram	6	4	10
Tiram paṇ	5	7	12
Tiram paṇṇiyāl	5	6	11
Tiram tirāttiram	5	4	9
Tirāttiram pan	4	7	11
Tirāttiram paṇṇiyāl	4	6	10
Tirāttiram tiram	4	5	9

Aruti — A theme is said to begin in Aruti when its starting point is at the end of the prior Āvarta.

Āvarta — A complete time-measure. Time taken for executing the constituent aṅgas of a tāḷa once (Tāḷa āvarta).

Gati — Rate in akāras per kriyā at which letters of an expression or series of śabdas (percussion sounds) keep on progressing. It is of five kinds, the rate of movement being 4, 3, 7, 5 and 9 ākāras respectively per kriyā.

Jāti — Rhythmical solfa syllables called 'Pātam' in Sanskrit and 'Śolkaṭṭu' in Tamil.

Jāti — One of the ten elements in musical time refers to five varieties of 'Laghu'.

Kaṭṭaḷai — The exact import of the Tamil word is very much in debate.

Kauttuvam — An invocation in Tamil in praise of deities, popularly used in dance recitals consists of Sāhitya and Jatis. 'Pañcha mūrti Kauttuvam' and 'Navasandhi Kauttuvam' are two branches. The former has the structure of Sanchārī gīta and the second of 'Iśai iḷakkaṇa gīta' Tanjore quartette made liberal use of them in temple-dance performances.

Index